Any Excuse
for a
PARTY

The story of my Life

Ange Hilstron

authorHOUSE®

AuthorHouse™ UK
1663 Liberty Drive
Bloomington, IN 47403 USA
www.authorhouse.co.uk
Phone: 0800 047 8203 (Domestic TFN)
         +44 1908 723714 (International)

Published by AuthorHouse 08/03/2019

ISBN: 978-1-7283-8644-7 (sc)
ISBN: 978-1-7283-8643-0 (e)

Print information available on the last page.

1

Chapter

I came into the world in August 1929, the year of the Wall Street Crash. My earliest memory of Christmas was my mother holding me in her arms as my father tied coloured balloons in the corners of the sitting room, getting ready for a Christmas party. I can still see his excited face and hear his laughter as he blew one up, let it go, and watched as it whirled around the room, making squeaking noises until it banged into a wall and sank to the floor. My parents were great party people. They entertained a lot and went to parties held on a riverboat moored on the Thames. They also attended dances in public dance halls. They loved dressing up for festive occasions and declared that one should always dress as if going to a party. This story is about turning points in my life that occurred during the festive seasons.

Our Christmas decorations were lavish, brightly coloured paper swags, bells, and hangings that folded up when not in use. Intricate lace-paper bunting hung from the corners of the room to the central light fitting with bunches of holly and mistletoe. A large Norway spruce tree took pride of place, festooned with glass baubles resembling fruits. Red candles placed in candleholders were clipped on branches of the tree, and on Christmas Eve, when the candles were lit, we held hands to sing carols and dance around the room. The children's faces were bright with happiness and excitement for what was to come.

The Christmas cake and plum puddings had been prepared by hand months before. Everyone was involved in the preparation of ingredients for the puddings. Almonds were soaked in hot water to remove the skins before they were chopped. The raisins had their seeds removed. The beef suet was taken from around the kidneys. Breadcrumbs were shredded, and flour was sifted with mixed spices, cinnamon, and grated nutmeg. The eggs were whipped and citrus peel, sultanas, raisins, and currants were steeped in brandy. Finally, the whole lot was stirred together with a wooden spoon in a large earthenware mixing bowl. The barley wine was added, and a dash of rum was mixed in for good measure. Everyone had a turn in mixing the pudding, and one lucky child was then given the bowl to scrape clean and lick the spoon after the mixture had been placed into pudding bowls. After being covered in a cloth, the puddings were steamed for several hours and stored in the larder. A lucky silver coin wrapped in greased paper was inserted in the mixture when it was put into the pudding bowls as a surprise for someone eating the pudding.

The icing of the Christmas cake was also a special treat, with handmade almond icing. The almonds were prepared as before, but they were finely minced to make a paste. Once the cake had been stored for six months, holes were made in the top with a skewer, and sherry was poured into the holes. It was now ready for the almond paste to be spread, and the white royal icing was sculpted over the cake. This was lifted up with a fork to resemble snow, and small china characters of a snowman, a robin, a boy on a sled, and Father Christmas were placed amongst sprigs of holly and a bottlebrush fir tree. A large red ribbon was then tied around it, and the cake was placed on a decorative plate on the servery for afternoon tea, along with the mince pies, turkey sandwiches, ham pies, and chocolate truffles.

I was a picky eater. Because I was thin and highly strung, my mother thought I needed fatty food, but I was unable to digest it. It must have been at a family gathering at my grandparents' house, with family members all seated around a large table. Everyone wore funny paper hats and chatted animatedly to each other as Grandfather stood at the head of the table, carving the roast beef. I sat on a stool at the table instead of in my high chair. A plate of food was put in front of me, and a spoonful was put against my firmly closed mouth. True to form, I threw myself backwards to avoid having the spoon pushed into my mouth, and I landed on the floor.

It was in 1933 that the Great Depression, which was caused by the Wall Street Crash, began to bite, and my father became redundant. From then on, a series of events ensured that our lives would never be the same again. I do not remember many Christmases with my father's mother. However, on one enjoyable occasion near to Christmas, I was taken to visit Grandmother in her London flat. She was a stylish lady, with her hair in a chignon, and she wore woollen suits that she had knitted herself. I loved visiting her at her workplace. Once I was taken to watch the Lord Mayor's Show and the banquet below in the hall, where Grandfather and Grandmother had once been guests.

On this particular occasion, Father and I travelled by underground train and walked from the station to her flat. It had been fairly misty during the day, and now it threatened a pea-soup fog. With the smoke from coal fires, the air was full of choking sulphur, and we covered our faces with scarves to keep out the fumes. People were scurrying about, dressed in long overcoats and wearing galoshes over their shoes. A horse and cab trotted past, and chestnuts roasting on a brazier in the gutter attracted a crowd. A man with a monkey stood on the pavement under a gas street light outside her building, winding a barrel organ that played a jolly tune. Passers-by threw coins into a hat at his side each time the monkey danced up and down to the tune.

We climbed up the stairs to Grandmother's flat, and there she was, busy stirring the ingredients for Christmas puddings. A big bowl of raisins and sultanas soaking in brandy stood on the dining table. She lit the brandy, and blue flames leapt up. I was told that if I could retrieve as many raisins as I could before the flames died, I could eat them. What an exciting game that was. I do not remember how many I ate, but it was fun trying to avoid burning my fingers.

She had a wonderful collection of all kinds of musical boxes. Some were very large, with big brass barrels studded with pins that played music hall tunes. Others were tiny wood boxes that tinkled a waltz or jig. There was a bird in a cage that moved around and sang, and automated figures that moved when wound up. I played with the silhouette theatre and made up my own Christmas story. A stage made of wood, with paper drapes, was unfolded, and a lit candle was put behind a white cloth hung behind the drapes. The characters on sticks were then placed between the light and the cloth, throwing shadows on the cloth. The sticks could be moved about, creating a dramatic effect, or remain in a still tableau. There were box dioramas and cardboard Shakespeare theatres in her collections, as well as various doll's houses and contents. There were peep shows and magic lantern shows as well. Grandmother taught me to do eyelet embroidery on handkerchiefs as presents for Christmas, introducing me to a love of needlework. Although she was a prodigious knitter, she never taught me how to knit.

It must have been about this time that my mother, brother, and I were invited to a party at her father's place. I remember sitting on the ballroom floor, in a party dress and with a lot of other excited children, in front of a massive Christmas tree festooned with sparkling decorations. Gifts were handed out from the tree to eager children by a startling man with a long white beard and dressed in a long red coat. Paper wrappings were strewn across the floor as the presents were unwrapped and shown to happy parents. It was such a joyous and surprising occasion that it has stayed in my memory all these years.

We always put a pillowcase at the end of the bed for Father Christmas to fill with small gifts. I usually had a dressed doll of some kind or a soft toy animal. I did not like dolls because they were made of wax or celluloid that melted if left in front of a fire. China dolls were popular then, with moving eyes and limbs, and sometimes the bodies were made of composite materials that disintegrated when left in the bath. Inevitably, I would drop a china doll, and it would smash. Unknown to me, my mother had spent hours making and knitting doll's clothes, which I immediately ripped off, never to put them back on again. In fact, I much preferred the engines and carriages with the rails that my brother had, or the trucks filled with sweets.

During my early years, we hardly seemed to spend very long at any address, yet there was always a celebration on Christmas Day, with carols at church and a hearty dinner. In those days, a piece of roast beef or chicken was a treat, surrounded by a mix of various vegetables and stuffing. However, Christmas pudding was always the highlight, dowsed in brandy and lit as it came from the kitchen to the table. One lucky person would take a mouthful to discover a silver sixpence hidden in it. There were special table fireworks and strange pieces of fabric that, when lit, turned into black oozing monsters. There were always nuts to crack, oranges found at the bottom of our pillowcases, and dolly mixtures.

2

Chapter

The culmination of our wanderings occurred when we found ourselves homeless. My mother took my brother and me to the park, where she sat on a bench until the park-keeper came to tell her at closing time that it was time to leave. He contacted the Salvation Army to find us lodgings, and a kind family offered their sofa, where we could sleep for the night. My mother found a typing job and arranged to rent a room upstairs from the family. She also asked the lady if she would give my brother and me an evening meal. We lived there for several months, during which I also contracted chickenpox and was enrolled in the Roman Catholic school. My mother had taught me how to read and write, and I did not start school until I was six.

I met children at school who were having a party. My party dress was altered slightly to fit, and there we stood at the front door with my hair curled up to look like Shirley Temple. They were in the middle of party games: Hunt the Thimble, Blind Man's Bluff, and Squeak Piggy Squeak (where guests were being blindfolded while sitting on a cushion on someone's lap and guessing who it was). I was not included in the game of Sardines, where people squashed into tight places in and under beds and inside wardrobes.

Life seemed to improve miraculously after we settled into our new address. Christmas presents became larger and did not fit the pillowcases left for Father Christmas to fill. I had large storybooks of fairy tales and *Playbox* annuals while my brother had *Beano* and boys' stories. One Christmas I found a very large baby doll at the bottom of my bed that I kept for years, even after I had my own daughter. Another time, I was given a bicycle, and my brother got a tricycle. My father taught us how to ride them.

My father had more time to spend with us, and we used to go on picnics in the Essex countryside or up to the coast. We visited my aunt and uncle in Surrey, as well as their three boys who seemed to be very excitable. They always had a big party on Boxing Day, and the boys could not resist licking the Christmas cake icing and the cream off the trifle. Father Christmas brought them wood bricks for building castles, tin soldiers, and spitting fiery tanks. I was very envious of these.

My uncle was very fond of party games, and we played My Grandfather's Nose, which was a remembering game, and Consequences, where people wrote down answers to questions, folded over the page, and passed it to the next person, ending in 'And the consequence was ...' Then the page was read out. We played the usual magic guessing games and lifted a person in a chair using two fingers. I seem to recall that the trick was to press down on the person's head, place a finger under an armpit and knee, and lift them up. It required two people to do it. There were laughing games where one side laughed to make the others laugh, and a spittle fly game where someone was asked what kind of fly they were. Other people were outside the room and so could not see what was going on. When it came to the last person in the line, they said they were a spittle fly and threw a thimbleful of water over the person who asked the question; then they joined the line and became the spittle fly for the next person entering the room.

This was followed by a sumptuous feast and presents handed out from beneath the tree. Every Boxing Day, my aunt played the piano and was joined by my mother in a duet. Mother usually gave a rendition of 'Little Orphan Annie' or some other piece to make our skin crawl. She would unexpectedly launch into the room with wide eyes and dramatic gestures to give her version of 'The Boy Stood on the Burning Deck' or

'The Highwayman'. We were encouraged to do party pieces but were often too shy.

The years 1936 and 1937 were halcyon days with long, hot summers. My brother and I joined a swimming club at the city swimming pool, where we obtained rosettes for swimming skills. We both went to the pool every day for swimming lessons after school and played around in the cold pool after standing under the hot showers. I started to learn how to dive and was soon on the springboards and the top board. Although I could swim, I much preferred diving and underwater swimming, so I was put on the synchronised swimming team and was coached for diving. I contracted mumps and measles, which put an end to that idea. As things turned out, our fortunes were to change rapidly during the next two years, but for now we were a happy family.

3

Between 1937 and the beginning of 1939, there were the stirrings of something terrible about to happen. However, as a seven- and eight-year-old, life appeared to be full of exciting new discoveries. I went to school on the tram that clattered past our furniture shop, and I fell in love with the conductor who looked like a cowboy film star. I explored the back roads on my bike, discovered the water pumping station with its huge driving belt, and stood on the overbridge at the railway station in the belching smoke from the engine. I watched the Black Shirts marching down High Street, as well as men and boys doing exercises in the schoolyard. I was used as a guinea pig for diphtheria inoculations, and one of my classmates died from the disease. I was taken into town by my mother to see *Snow White* at the cinema for a Christmas treat, and my boyfriend tried to kiss me behind the rhododendrons in the park. I took my first Holy Communion dressed in my white ribbon flounced party dress and a white veil, and my father bought me a locket of Saint Veronica to celebrate.

We sat in the back kitchen of the shop having breakfast and listening to the radio on a sunny September morning in 1939. We had eaten our wheat flakes and cold milk and were waiting for the bacon and eggs frying on the gas cooker. A very severe-sounding announcer stated on the radio that Britain was now at war with Germany. No sooner had he finished explaining why than the air raid siren went off at the fire station nearby. We sat miserably in the next-door air raid shelter with our feet in rainwater until the all-clear sounded.

Although it seemed a sudden decision to go to war, there had been preparations going on for months before. Men were being drilled and called up long before to create a reserve army to help prevent the insurgence of German Armed Forces in Europe. Some were already fighting in France and Belgium to little avail. We had been issued gas masks and given registration numbers, and arrangements had been made to evacuate key government departments to bunkers outside London and children into country areas away from possible harm. Ration books were handed out in case of food shortages. Fleets of merchant ships were reassigned to shipping essentials in the North Sea. Small arms factories were hastily reassembled from making home products. Farmers were given orders to grow more food.

My mother had already packed suitcases for this eventuality, and arrangements were made for her, my brother, and me to stay with a family friend in Somerset. Father hastily handed us bacon sandwiches through the taxi window that was to take us to the railway station. He promised to visit us as soon as he had wound up his businesses and stored our goods. Apparently, he had been called up to work in an aircraft factory because he was too old to join the Forces.

My mother's sister and her three boys were already settled with another family friend on a farm, and the two older boys were attending the school there. We were invited to the end-of-year Christmas school concert at the local village hall. The hall was crowded with locals, as well as people from far and wide, including the new intake of evacuees looking very lonely and out of place. The concert opened with rousing World War I songs, and then a jolly boy with a ruddy face sang 'Run Rabbit Run' and invited us to join in. Then there was a song about the Siegfried Line that deserved a thunderous applause, with everyone cheering and clapping. There was a Christmas tableau with the Three Kings, and various children dressed up as Joseph and Mary, angels, animals, and the star of Bethlehem; a cot with a baby doll in it represented Jesus.

To end, there was a mummers' play with St George killing the dragon. The dragon was brought back to life by the local doctor, who pulled a string of sausages out of its stomach. What an exciting evening it was, followed by a table of pies and cakes baked by the farmers' wives and the parents of the schoolchildren. I seem to remember a game of Musical Chairs and Pass the Parcel somewhere in the mix, but that might have been at another Christmas party at someone's farmhouse.

The lady we stayed with was very slim and straight, and she wore her grey hair in a tight bun in the nape of her neck. Her dress was a Liberty print of tiny flowers with a small collar buttoned right up to her chin. She lived in a three-storey red brick detached cottage on a lane at the far end of the village. My bedroom was up in the attic, with a sloping ceiling, a rag rug on the wood floor, and a big oak wardrobe. There was a washstand with a basin and jug, a chamber pot under the bed, and a feather and straw mattress with a knitted coverlet. I immediately felt at home. In winter, the windows and bed cover were sprinkled with frost. The water in the jug under the washstand was a block of ice, but it all added to the mystery.

The downstairs front parlour was only opened on a Sunday. Hymns were played on a very out-of-tune piano. The back kitchen, with its iron coal range and black kettle steaming on the hob, was the centre of the household. A rocking chair placed by the open fire soon became Mother's favourite place to sit. Oil lamps lit the rooms, and candles lit us to bed. There was an outside earth closet with newspaper hung on a string, as well as a mains water tap for drinking at the side of the building. A pump to draw water from the well stood by the back door, and a rainwater butt was placed under the eaves for the laundry and hair washing. Any trash from the house, including sewage, was thrown over the boundary hedge onto a farm midden to be spread on the fields. A tin bath hung on the back door, and we bathed in it in front of the range once a week; the dirty water tipped out in the yard by the well.

Fresh skimmed milk and clotted cream was collected in billy cans and jugs from a farm down a very muddy lane. My brother and I sloshed down there in our Wellington boots after school to collect it. A couple of ladies sold us fresh eggs farther along the lane. One of the ladies with hair like a bird's nest held a trumpet shape to her ear so she could hear me. One day she told me that they were not allowed to sell eggs anymore; they were sent to a factory to be dried instead. Vegetables were home-grown in the large cottage garden, as well as damsons and soft fruits. I remember Sweet William flowers growing beside the garden path. The orange lantern plants and silver seed pods, made into dried flower Christmas arrangements, grew amongst them along with other cottage garden plants. Every inch of ground was productive with herbs and nasturtiums clambering in profusion. Meat, not yet rationed, was delivered by a local farmer who butchered his own animals.

I and my brother attended the village school, run by a single teacher. Children of all ages from four years old to twelve attended. I was the eldest girl at age ten, and the eldest boy was twelve. I learned more at that school than at any other. When I finished my lessons, I was co-opted to teach the younger pupils. I was also sent outside to prepare the soil for seeds, feed the chickens with dandelion leaves, make notes about the weather, and pick caterpillars off the cabbages. I wrote the school Christmas play for the teacher's entertainment. The children who grew up on farms and knew all about birth and how babies were formed were greatly amused by my version of an angel bringing the baby Jesus to Mary and putting him in the manger.

We were shown how to make large envelopes from art paper and decorate them with finely cut paper snow and cut-out pictures from old Christmas cards. We gave them in with our names on them and received them back again at the end of the term filled with things the teacher had collected from cereal and sample packets through the year. I had a retractable circular lace-making tool, a cotton reel knitting spool, a packet of sweets, and a small block of milk chocolate. There were instructions on how to make pom-poms for Christmas decorations. I cannot remember whether the cottage was decorated or whether we even had a tree, but we had wonderful dinners at the farm with my aunt and cousins and the farmer's family and friends.

We were invited to a Boxing Day party at a farm on the edge of a moor where a big battle had once been fought. I was taken to see the foxhound puppies in the barn—such beautiful little bundles with round tummies and smelling that sweet sour smell of dog and milk. Two large boys appeared carrying rifles and a brace of pheasants. In the evening after a stupendous Boxing Day feast, we played a hilarious game where I and another person hid under a blanket and were thwacked with a rolled newspaper. The aim was to guess who did it, but also it enabled the adults to engage in a bit of kissing and cuddling under the blanket.

That spring in 1940, there was a huge snowstorm with drifts reaching the height of the tall hedges. We had to dig out a path to the school cottage so that the teacher could get out, and school was closed until the thaw. Farmers who did not like the idea of these new-fangled tractors were pleased to have kept their shire horses. Our local butcher still used his pony and trap for deliveries. I watched while the sheep were dagged and tar was put on their hooves. I held the tails of the cows when they were milked and was told it would make the milk flow faster if I pumped the tail up and down.

We had helped to pick up apples in the cider apple orchards for the press in the autumn, and we tied and placed the stooks in the wheat fields. We bounced on the hay carts and helped to lift the bundles of hay onto the rick. I was taught how to swing a scythe in a slow, even movement, as well as how to knead bread from the ground wheat. I learned to read the clouds to forecast the weather and watch the leaves on trees turn towards a stormy sky. I learned to tell the difference between a rabbit and a hare, a blackbird and a starling, and a rook and a jackdaw. I could identify the different herbs that grew in the hedgerows.

That spring, we were apprehended by a gamekeeper after my mother climbed through a fence to pick primroses and violets growing in the spinney by the fields near the cottage. No amount of appeal would persuade him to allow us to go farther. We were told to get off his land.

4

My father came to visit bringing belated Christmas parcels, which we opened right away. I do not remember what presents I was given, but we were sent into the parlour to play while he and my mother talked. Apparently there was no sign of the war starting, and everything seemed safe in spite of propaganda to the contrary. It seemed pointless for us to be hiding away down in the West Country when we could all be together. My aunt and cousins had already returned home to Surrey, and Mother wanted to go back to be near her. Father said he would try to find a house to rent somewhere in the vicinity.

The house my father chose was semi-detached in a development by the railway line. It was beside a huge electricity pylon and was the ugliest place I had ever seen. The contrast between here and the country idyll was enormous—and had it been realised, it was right on the bombing path to London. However, it was within easy distance of my aunt's place, on the edge of countryside then, with a small stream a walk away. It was also close to where I was enrolled in a small private school that both my mother and grandmother had attended.

We watched the Battle of Britain in our back garden, marvelling at the airplanes weaving in and out in intricate manoeuvres, some spiralling down with smoke pouring from them. My mother said it was a dogfight, little realising its importance. We put crisscrossed paper on windows in case of bomb blasts and made the downstairs toilet and cupboard under the stairs as places to shelter from air raids. Blackout curtains were up, and my father tried to dig through the hard clay in the back garden to make a shelter. He was working as a toolmaker at an aircraft factory. While coming downstairs about to catch the coach, there was a tremendous crash, and he fell the rest of the way. The siren sounded, and an anti-aircraft gun towed by an engine on the railway opened fire. Such a thunderous noise had us in hysterics as we huddled into the downstairs toilet until the all-clear sounded. This was the first introduction to a continuous bombardment that lasted for fifty-seven days and nights from September 1940 to May 1941, as a softening up to German invasion.

That Christmas I discovered there was no such thing as Father Christmas and that it was my parents who'd filled the pillowcases with presents. I was unable to sleep while listening to my father changing radio channels in the sitting room below. He had been a radio cadet when young and knew Morse Code, so he hoped to pick up news being broadcast in Code. I wandered down the stairs, hoping to be given a cup of cocoa to help me sleep, and found my mother and father in the kitchen. He was sitting on the floor and putting finishing touches to a twig thatched cottage.

I had asked Father Christmas for a set of farm animals made of metal, and here was my father making the barns and hedge and painting the windows on a cottage. My mother was painting a wood truck and trailer for my brother. They said that Father Christmas had asked them to help because he was caught up in the war, but they would give them to him when they were finished. I pretended to be happy with that idea. I was not surprised to find a farm set up under the Christmas tree with the cottage and farm animals in fenced fields. Over the years, the animals' legs bent or broke off, but I still managed to keep a few until I downsized a few years ago.

There was the threat of invasion by Germany, and my parents were told by the Government to ask any overseas family members if they would take my brother and me as evacuees for the duration of the war.

We were all ready with suitcases under our beds to catch the next sailing when the ship sailing before ours was torpedoed in the Atlantic with great loss of young life, so our sailing was cancelled. Mother, feeling she could not live without children in the house, became pregnant, and Father went on night duty at the factory. He was working on a system to do with night flying, later known as Radar. My sister was born in 1941 during a savage bombing raid.

After the devastation of London Blitz in 1940–41 with the sky lit up like an enormous fireworks display, my grandmother's flat was destroyed. She came to live with us for a while in the front bedroom until some other place could be found for her out of harm's way. We had sat on the floor in the assembly room at school to hear about the Dunkirk rescue of our troops and sang 'For Those in Peril on the Sea'. Now at the height of daylight raids, we sought shelter in the school basement and sang 'Onward Christian Soldiers'. My exams were interrupted by air raids, and visits to the basement shelters were a welcome distraction. After a while, we became accustomed to the night bombings and gave up seeking shelter in the underground public shelters; my mother said she preferred to die in her own bed. I only remember being really frightened once, when bombs started to fall really close with screamers attached to them. We became philosophical after a while and thought that if this was how we were going to die, then so be it. For children, it became an adventurous way of life, avoiding being caught and looking for keepsakes in the rubble. Each morning my brother and I went out to pick up the lumps of shrapnel from bursting anti-aircraft shells, and we'd gape at the rubble of people's homes that littered the street.

5

Chapter

Christmas 1941 was bleak. Rationing was in full swing, and all kinds of restrictions were put on food and luxury products. At school, the head teacher encouraged us to adopt an American pen friend. I still send her Christmas cards and letters, but then we exchanged stories of our lives, and she sent our family Lease Lend parcels. American soldiers were stationed in the market town close by, and Canadian soldiers were hiding in the woods around Surrey. We made Christmas decorations by folding strips of coloured paper and looping them together in a chain. My mother bought a tree in a plant pot, and we painted it with flour and water to look like snow. A few baubles saved from other Christmases and presents hidden in the branches completed the decorations. I made a rag doll for my sister out of an old sock, and Mother pulled back the wool from an old sweater and knitted a new one for me.

We hosted our first Boxing Day party, and a few of my mother's relatives arrived with gifts and offers of help. Amongst them were cousins, both talented artists, who were working with the Americans. They invited me to stay in their flat overlooking a tributary of the Thames and go to the Music Hall Pantomime. Although my school often took us to the theatre to see the ballet, I had never been to a Pantomime before, and it was a complete riot with audience participation and gender swaps, such wonderful costumes and scenery, and comedy with joyful songs and dances to lift our spirits. I often stayed with these delightful relatives. They had marvellous collections of art books and classical records that were a lasting influence on my love of art.

By 1942 the Blitz was easing, and Germany had transferred its attention to conquering Russia. However, another horror of flying bombs was yet to come. Now a single parent permanently separated from my Father, my Mother was struggling to pay my school fees. My brother had finished attending the Preparatory School and was enrolled in the Boys' Comprehensive School. It was suggested that my fees be reduced, and I would be trained as a student teacher at my school. I had enormous potential, although no one ever told me in what. I had already passed the Teachers College preliminary examination and was about to take Junior Oxford School Certificate. I had also an Art Bursary through art examinations I had taken, and I needed only one more examination to gain enough points to teach. However, once again events intervened with the barrage of unmanned flying bombs being launched relentlessly on civilian areas.

The school decided to evacuate to a safer area, and the Head suggested that I should go with them. Instead, my Mother withdrew me from school, and at the age of almost fourteen, I stayed at home to look after my brother and baby sister while she went out to work. Wartime Christmases were still celebrated, but gone was the pudding, to be replaced with gelatine fruit trifle made with bottled or tinned fruit. During the year, we were sent out to bombed sites to scrump blackcurrants or plums from back gardens, and we'd collect twigs and bits of broken timbers for kindling. Eggs and milk were powdered, and butter was mixed with margarine for shortening and spread on bread. We had always been used to having a meagre diet, but now we were starving.

About twenty or so flying bombs were dropping every minute. By now my mother was working at her father's place after a period of helping in a school. At age fifteen, I began as a shorthand typist at a Shipping Agency in the City. It was soon discovered I was hopeless at both shorthand and typing. In fact, I really was not suited to office work at all.

A cold ground mist swirled around my ankles as I walked slowly down the lane to the railway station. Grandfather had bought me my first pair of heeled shoes to go to work, and they caused nasty blisters on my heels. It took the electric train twenty minutes to get to Waterloo Station. I enjoyed the excitement of navigating through crowds of passengers to get to the underground City Line. There was always a crush in the spacious lift that took us down to the Underground, where there were further escalators and corridors to stations. The City tube train ran underneath the River Thames to the other side. While coming out from beneath the depths on my way to the office, I found a rubber road full of horses and black bank carriages and men wearing top hats, while men with reinforced bowler hats and umbrellas scurried past the blackened buildings.

The Dickensian building where I was to work was bitterly cold in winter. The lift was operated by an old, hunchbacked, wizened man pulling on a rope hand pulley. At the dark and dingy third floor, we finally reached our front office. A tall counter separated the office staff from customers, behind which sat a tall, whiskered man with a high Edwardian collar who was an Insurance broker and a pale, straight-haired lady munching cheese sandwiches. She seemed to make them last all day. It was she who managed the books, answered the switchboard, and typed a few letters. I was the owner's secretary, but as I have said, I was hopeless at it. I could take shorthand with speed, but I memorised what had been said rather than read it back. I made terrible typing mistakes as well, with smudges all over the page, rubbing them out. I was also not all that good at operating the switchboard.

In final desperation, I was given the job as a Runner, taking documents to various City buildings. I loved it, finding my way down alleys and round corners with no maps and ending up in some fascinating street in the City. My favourite place was a building with the revolving doors operated by a waterwheel. The main foyer displayed large glass cabinets with detailed models of cruise liners. My job was to take the vast United States Entry Application forms to the Outgoing Passengers clerk. The only means of transport then was by ship. Afterwards, I would find my way to the Monument, by the fish market, or to the flower, fruit, and vegetable market. At Christmas during the war, barrow boys pushed their carts laden with fruit through the City and sold their produce to the office workers at lunchtime and before going home from work. They were often moved on by police for causing an obstruction. Men with suitcases surreptitiously sold the contents in alleyways, usually stuff that was stolen or on the Black Market. They had lookouts who warned them if the police were checking on them, and they folded up their cases and disappeared into the crowd, often forgetting to give change.

People worked up until noon on Christmas Eve and Christmas Day and Boxing Day were taken as holidays. Christmas decorations were put up on Christmas Eve and often taken down again after Boxing Day. A potted Norway spruce was generally bought by my Mother from the market, along with sprigs of holly and mistletoe. After Christmas, the tree was planted in the garden for the following year, or stuffed up the chimney and set alight to clean the soot from the flue. Invariably, the chimney stack would catch alight, and my Mother would throw salt on the embers and hang a wet sack in front of the fireplace. Great wads of flaming soot would fall into the hearth, to be scooped up and put on the garden flower beds to kill the slugs. Nothing was wasted.

By now the Allied Forces had invaded Europe, and we saw convoys of trucks, gun carriers, and troops nose to tail along our main roads. We watched tanks thundering down the bypass. We watched in awe as huge formations of Flying Fortress bombers flew overhead. Still in formation, they returned home with equally large gaps where the aircraft had been shot down. We were still being bombarded by V-2 rockets, but the sudden silence and lack of guns and siren warnings was almost an anticlimax. I could understand how soldiers, having been on the front line and in fear of death, felt unable to settle at home. I listened to the American Forces Network on the radio and danced around the room to Glen Miller and his band. American comedians joined us on the radio at Sunday lunch, and we listened to *Children's Hour* at teatime. We listened to the King's stammered Christmas message, willing him to finish his words.

My mother encouraged me to give my Notice at the shipping agency and introduced me to a man who had been an executive at a cigarette and tobacco manufacturing firm. He was staying at my grandfather's place, and he kindly gave me a letter of introduction to a colleague. This turn of events was to alter my life in unexpected ways.

6
Chapter

The impressive building was built in 1913 on the corner of two main roads in the Beaux Arts style with imposing Italianate facades, and it was part of a group of Imperial houses along the length of the street opposite the river. A liveried doorman took my letter of introduction at the entrance, guided me up to the wood-panelled and carpeted third floor, and passed the letter on to a Commissionaire. After a short wait, I was taken into an inner office to be greeted by the Assistant Manager and was engaged as a shorthand typist. It was soon realised that I was not very good at it, and they made me a teleprinter operator instead.

On Christmas Eve, there was an office party. A lady selling hand-knit Fairisle gloves, Nylon underwear, and Christmas trinkets went around filling orders. A man from another department gave out tickets to London shows, and he distributed brightly coloured Turkish cigarettes and luxury lipsticks to a favoured few. I was lucky enough to be given tickets to see *Carousel, Annie Get Your Gun,* and *South Pacific,* as well as tickets for single acts including Judy Garland, Danny Kaye and Frank Sinatra. Another Department Head shared big boxes of dried fruit from the Middle East. I bought a large bag of mandarins from the barrow parked in the street outside our building, as well as a large bunch of flowers from the florist on Waterloo Station. I felt elated with the expectant buzz, with people trying to get home in time to decorate the Christmas tree and prepare for Christmas Day.

By now the war was coming to an end, and we looked forward to the end of rationing. It became my job to decorate the Christmas tree, and over the years we'd collected some beautiful glass baubles. They had to be stored very carefully because they were very fragile. Often the clips attached to the top of each bauble would loosen, and the glass would shatter as soon as it touched the floor. Some of the pieces had belonged to my grandfather, and after his death, Mother had rescued them and other decorations from a cupboard. I loved the lead-up to Christmas with the sharp winter air and roaring fires. I revelled in the whole magic of the Season plus the excitement of surprise on Christmas morning. I loved visiting neighbours, singing carols, wrapping up in large overcoats and jerseys. I enjoyed choosing gifts and wrapping them in fancy paper late at night. I loved the bright displays in shop windows and the smell of roasting chestnuts on braziers in the marketplace. We watched the wonderful firework display on VE Day from the seventh floor of the building. The streets were full of people laughing and cheering as fire barges anchored in the middle of the river spouted jets of water, which were backlit by streaming fireworks. I watched ice hockey with my boyfriend and we went to the cinemas in town after eating baked beans on toast at a well-known restaurant. I remained working as teleprinter operator and part-time switchboard operator for several years.

Our family Christmas parties became more lavish and sophisticated, with bottles of sherry and cherry brandy. During my early teenage years, the young people were sent into the back room to listen to records on a wind-up gramophone and play card games; the adults sat in the front room and caught up with family news. My aunt and uncle still held their annual Boxing Day get-together, and my brother, fancying himself as a student of Upmanship, made plonking remarks to the older generation. He was soon to be called up into the Air Force. My sister was now old enough to attend a Convent School.

By the early fifties, our office had been moved into temporary accommodation in the grounds of a mansion house in Surrey. I went to work on a Company coach that stopped at the end of our road. It was as

I was alighting the coach for the journey home that my future husband glimpsed my ankles and determined to meet me.

I had known several young men previously, but it was never serious. During that period, most of the males of around the age of eighteen were conscripted for two years into the Armed Forces, so those left behind were either too young or too old for my generation to date. I had noticed this young man who, in the company of others, was being tutored as a Trainee Manager for one of the overseas locations. Their classroom was opposite the teleprinter desks where I worked. He finally plucked up courage to ask me out, and I was invited to spend Christmas with his family up North. I was greeted with love and affection and shown into my sumptuous bedroom where a fire was blazing in the hearth. His parents were like characters out of *The Darling Buds of May*. Full of warmth and bon viveur, his father was of French origin, and his mother was a buxom lady and great provisioner.

Everything was supersize. A huge Christmas tree stood in the corner of the sitting room decorated with lavish hangings and paper swags. Large bowls of fruit and nuts were on the table in front of a roaring fire. The dining table set in front of an Aga range in the farmhouse kitchen was laden with all kinds of vegetables in enormous covered tureens, and the roasted goose sat in pride of place to be carved by the head of the family. It was like something out of *A Christmas Carol*. Father tucked a napkin into his collar, and after he cut the goose, we offered our plates to be filled. He preferred to cut his vegetables into small pieces first before eating the meat. After eating second and third helpings of a generous portion of Christmas pudding, the family consumed several bananas and then demanded tea and Christmas cake. I had never seen so much food eaten at once. My boyfriend's mother said I was too thin, and she was alarmed by my small appetite.

My boyfriend finished his term of training and was posted to a factory up North to experience the manufacturing process of cigarette production. He came down by coach every other weekend to visit, and by the end of the year we were engaged. We went to concerts at the Albert Hall, saw the Diagelev Exhibition, watched the Coronation of Queen Elizabeth, and attended the Britain Can Make It Exhibition. I was taken to rugby matches and to local dance halls, and just before he was sent to East Africa for a three-year contract, we toured the South of England in his car.

7

Chapter

My fiancé went to work in a cigarette factory in Uganda. There was a Kikuyu uprising in Kenya about the same time, and the London head office became aware that there needed to be some changes made. The native staff were being trained in the running of the Colonial factories in preparation for a possible bid for Independence. After serving for a couple of years, during which time the Ugandan Kabaka was sent to England with his retinue, my fiancé decided to return home. We were married on New Year's Day 1955 and took up residence in a furnished flat in the suburbs. He applied for a salesman job and I continued to work for my company, which had moved back to Town.

Christmases were spent alternating between my family and my husband's family. The Festive Season remained as it had during the war with Christmas Eve (half-day), Christmas Day, and Boxing Day as holidays, so the trip by car up North was overnight. The main roads were two cars wide. There were no motorways then, and our small Ford Popular managed to make an average speed of forty miles an hour. Wrapped in warm clothing and rugs, we bumped along the darkened roads, struggling to keep awake. With an occasional comfort stop at convenient public houses on the way, we finally reached Scotch Corner in time for a meal.

I loved streaking through tunnels of trees outlined in the headlights and watching rabbits and bats scattering in the glare. Every village green had a lighted Christmas tree, and church stained-glass windows showed streaks of colour as we passed. Christmas lights shone brightly in cottage windows, and the crisp air fogged up the car windows as we crossed the Yorkshire Dales. My husband's Mother and Father met us nearer to their town to guide us home to warm by the Aga with a cup of hot chocolate before tumbling into bed.

My husband was transferred to the Midlands after a short training at an iron casting factory. He found a very pleasant one-bedroom furnished flat; it was in an attic with sloping ceilings and dormer windows. It seemed strange being so far away from my family, but we soon made friends with other flat dwellers. Our close neighbour was a Danish girl with her husband and two small children. Just before Christmas, she asked me to join her in the Festival of Lights. She wore a white gown and a crown of lighted candles on her fair head. We paraded around her flat while she sang Danish chants beneath a star-shaped light shade. At Christmas, we were invited to a combined party in one of the downstairs flats owned by a disabled man and his second wife. He had been a pilot injured in the war, and she was his nurse. When my husband went away on business, this couple asked me to stay. I used to get spooked living on my own in an old house, but after a while I became used to it.

I went to work for a Building Contractor at a very large building site as a Girl Friday. I had sole charge of the office staff and looked after the Quantity Surveyors, the Site Manager, and the Architect. For the very first time, I felt appreciated, and at Christmas I was presented with a bunch of roses, a box of chocolates, and a bottle of the best sherry.

After a while, my husband decided to look for another place to live, and we explored the wonderful countryside South of the large Midlands town. After walking around cosy lanes and looking at expensive houses in purpose-built villages, we came across a new development being built in a small hamlet. He picked a quarter-acre plot and a builder willing to build to our design. The two-storey detached house was ready by the following Christmas. The big Laboratory buildings were almost complete with the final painting of a large mural on the canteen wall. I began to feel it was time to give up work, and I wanted to enjoy my home. Everyone came to say farewell, and the Architect and Clerk of Works said that a job was there at the Head Office if I ever needed one.

My husband and I had always owned dogs, so he thought it would be nice to have a Gordon Setter pup. On a trip down South, he came across a woman who bred the dogs and had several puppies for sale. Our dog's kennel name was Treetops Chevalier, but we renamed him Baron. He was a remarkably intelligent and beautiful animal. Even though we never exhibited him in dog shows, he won a Reserve at Crufts, and the breeder hoped we would breed from him. We never did.

We got to know several people who bred dogs and realised that it was both time-consuming and expensive. One couple we became close to bred boxers and Siamese cats and owned a boarding kennels for dogs and cats. At one time, they had run a restaurant that had become so famous they'd had to give it up. They specialised in T-bone steak; garlic, olive oil, and greens salad; and American fried chicken in a basket at a time when nothing like it had been seen before. This couple had to work hard looking after the kennels over Christmas, so I cooked a turkey, and we took it over to their cottage to eat in the evening; she made a delicious pumpkin pie to go with the turkey.

We used to holiday in Cornwall in an ancient bed and breakfast cottage, in a seaside location. The lady had married a Cornish fisherman when she was a Land Girl during the war. They had a Jersey house-cow that she milked to make clotted cream and butter, and they grew anemones for the Covent Garden market. They did not have children, so they regarded us as their family. Every Christmas they sent us a pottle of clotted cream and a large bunch of mixed anemones. I have such wonderfully fond memories of these kind people, and I was greatly influenced by her style of hospitality. Whilst on holiday there, we bought a Siamese kitten that we named Kali Sana. I often took both Baron and Kali out for walks across the fields and by the meres.

8

Chapter

As I was looking out of the window one day, I saw a little girl toddling down the lane dressed in a flounced pinafore. Suddenly I felt the urge to have a baby of my own. Our baby daughter was born on a very foggy day in November 1957. She was the first girl to be born for generations in my husband's family. I had joined a craft club at the local village hall, where we made Christmas table decorations and kissing bunches out of woven willow twigs. Decorated with ribbons and sprigs of holly, the bunch was hung from the ceiling with mistletoe placed in the centre. I'd cut a branch of hazel whilst walking the dog, and I painted it white. The twigs were ideal places from which to hang Christmas cards. I placed a small Christmas tree laden with glass baubles on the shelf between the dining alcove and the sitting room. All the preparations were made for my Mother and sister to visit us. It was a very special occasion for them to see the new baby and enjoy the season with our little family.

I took my daughter to a toddler group in the village hall. There was a Paediatrician and Health Care nurse in attendance, and bottles of concentrated orange juice, cod liver oil, and jars of malt were handed out to the parents. I enjoyed these sessions because it was a chance to meet other mothers. My neighbour was a new mother, and she and her husband shared babysitting with us. We became best of friends. I also belonged to the Country Women's Institute, which met once a month in the evening in the village hall, and I was chosen to take the lead in a play. I won several competitions for cake making and table decorations, and I became part of the team doing community work. Our area was classed as a hamlet, with a few cottages, a farm at the end of our lane, Council houses, and new private building developments by the railway. The village hall was the hub.

My husband said he yearned for the open spaces and lifestyle in Africa, and he had applied for several jobs in South Africa, hoping to get back into the tobacco industry. I was pregnant at the time with our daughter but wanted to have the baby in England. I was told that South Africa had the very best hospitals, but I was adamant she should be born in England. His brother wrote home from New Zealand with glowing colours, showing photos of modern buses and open-plan homes. We were interviewed at New Zealand House for immigration, where we were told that we were not the usual candidates. They were looking for carpenters and builders, and we were too well educated so would not fit in. My husband's brother said he would sponsor us, and we were booked on the *Arcadia*, leaving in May and arriving in New Zealand on 12 July 1960. I felt terribly unhappy leaving our home and families and friends, but my husband was determined to go. We told our family and friends at Christmas of our intention to immigrate to New Zealand.

We had our home up for sale and were selling and giving away pieces of furniture and objects we could not pack in a small crate. We had to find a home for our animals. The Siamese had died a horrible death from rat poison, and the remaining one was taken by a girl down the Lane. Baron went to the breeder, who found him a home with a lady who owned a Gordon Setter bitch. Looking back, it was possibly a combination of reasons why my husband decided so strongly to leave. There had been a Strontium-90 leakage at a local atomic power station that had affected our milk supply. Russia was beginning to show signs of aggression with the possibility of atomic and chemical warfare against the United States. The market in iron goods was flagging, with steel manufacturing offshore. The European Union was making new trade rules, and eventually cast-iron products were not required anymore. In a short local newspaper article, my husband explained that England was getting too crowded.

9
Chapter

My mother said goodbye at her front gate. My husband's family said farewell to us on the boat train taking us to Dover. His Mother cried with agony of possibly never seeing her granddaughter again. We were hustled onto the cruise liner and shown our cabins in the bowels of the ship. Women and children were separated from the men. I and my two-year-old daughter shared a four-berth cabin with a woman and her teenage daughter. There were no portholes, but we had a very loud air conditioning unit. My husband shared with five other men in another six-berth cabin, farther down below decks. Most of the immigrant passengers were bound for Australia. Amongst the 350 children were some teenagers in charge of a group of orphans bound for foster homes in Australia.

With utter dismay, I realised that the ship was leaving port. The Cliffs of Dover faded into the distance without us knowing. I cannot fully express the enormous feeling of sorrow and loss I felt. My husband had hoped I would be delighted with the adventure once we set sail. Life on board was not ideal. Children ran all over the ship, the tar caulking on the decks stuck to clothing, children had to have their meals separately from adults, and the crèche for the little ones was right over the engine room. We left my daughter in the crèche only once. She was so distressed with the noise that we asked the family in the opposite cabin if we could share babysitting.

The Bay of Biscay was very rough, and most of the passengers were seasick. Our first port of call was Cairo, but because of the Egyptian war, we were unable to go ashore. We were in one of the last ships to go down the Suez Canal. It was fascinating to watch the desert life along the canal, with small villages and men riding camels and wearing black veils. We stopped at Aden and then at Ceylon, where we took a taxi to one of the small villages on the other side of the island. Children begging for money were shooed away by our driver, and we ended up having curry in the Governor's House. It took seven weeks to get to New Zealand, calling at Perth, Freemantle, Adelaide, Melbourne, and Sydney, where most of the immigrants disembarked. From then on, it became a cruise ship, and the attitude of the crew changed remarkably.

My husband's brother met us in Auckland, where we handed over our British Passports to officials. We were now potential New Zealand Citizens. We were taken on a whirlwind trip around the outskirts of the city and up into the highland bush. Booked on an overnight train with a sleeping cabin, we arrived early hours next morning to catch the ferry. We were exhausted by then with all the travelling, and we were totally unprepared for thick frost on the harbour wall. We arrived in July 1960, in the middle of winter, wearing summer clothing. There was a thick sea mist covering the winding cliff road out of the port. I have never felt so bereft as then. We stayed briefly at my brother-in-law's home, which tucked under a dark and imposing cliff at the back of a seaside township. He took us on a ride around industrial sites and proudly showed where his office was situated. Although he had sponsored my husband as an immigrant, it was expected that he would find another suitable job after a short while. It was obvious we could not remain as guests in their crowded home, so my husband went to find us a tiny seaside cabin on top of a sandhill.

We had spent the winter in a converted beach hut, during which time we had suffered from a type of tropical fever. My husband found a job as a Sales Representative with an oil company. My little daughter began wetting her bed, and I was dismayed by the backward and insular place to which we had been transported. It was nothing like the wonderful picture of modernity and space we had been led to believe. The dilapidated, tin-roof, lap-wood houses were crammed together. Telegraph poles leaning at odd angles lined the wide streets, carrying electricity and telephone wires and the odd street light. A shopping precinct was like a frontier town, with signage plastered on everything. The local food store was poorly stocked. I was amazed when the storekeeper whispered that a shipment of oranges and bananas had recently arrived. A windswept beach with huge grey volcanic sandhills stretched for miles, the crashing surf scouring the sand. No one went near it except a few brave boys on surf boards. The whole place was a deserted dump.

We moved to a cosier, furnished, two-bedroom chalet in a seaside township just before Christmas, a block away from the esplanade. Christmas in New Zealand coincides with summer holidays, so when we visited my brother-in-law, we found his wife busy ironing and preparing to go camping. Their Radiata pine branch was propped in the corner of the room, shedding its needles, the decorations dropping from wilted twigs. We were handed hastily wrapped presents and a mince pie while their boys bounced around the room. We had expected Christmas dinner on the beach as advertised by the authorities in Britain, but the weather was cold and windy, and most people went to their holiday houses or went camping in the bush over the holiday.

The lead-up to Christmas began with a business party for the children with Father Christmas sweltering in his costume. Presents, bought by the staff, were handed to the children, and the adults enjoyed drinks and titbits. At parties, the social custom was gender segregated, so the women sat drinking tea in the sitting room while the men stood drinking beer in the kitchen. Food was served late evening when the couples mingled together, careful not to be seen talking to someone else's husband or wife; for some curious reason, it was thought to be an invitation to an affair. It was something I could never get used to.

The great event before Christmas was an animated parade with floats through city streets. A large department store put on the show every year, providing most of the large figures and the animated reindeer for Father Christmas's sleigh. Carols by Candlelight was down by the

River on Christmas Eve. Singing carols and watching the lights flickering in the dusk brought tears to my eyes as I remembered how far we were from home and loved ones. I was homesick and unhappy, without any chance of ever returning to England.

10

Chapter

Concerned that I was not settling as he had hoped, my husband sought advice from friends, who suggested that I needed another child. I wanted to go home. There was nothing in this raw land that I could identify with, in spite of everyone telling me how lucky I was to be in God's own country. I was persuaded to send our daughter to attend play school in the village. Children from the age of two were expected to socialise with other children before going to kindergarten. The young woman in charge was very keen I should help with looking after the children, and I was introduced to other mothers. I soon made friends with several expat women who formed a committee for social evenings. These ladies were amongst the few parents to take an interest in the running of the play school, and they were instrumental in raising funds and providing resources for the school.

Now that we seemed to have a permanent home, I was anxious to have our dog, Baron, join us. I had given the breeder the money for his fare and awaited his arrival with anticipation. It took a long time for the breeder to agree to send him, and apparently the crew on the merchant ship were so scared of him that he remained in his crate on the deck for the whole of the five-week journey. The ship docked at port, and when we arrived to collect him, we found the crate had been shipped to the city with other goods to be sorted. We argued with the officials in the warehouse until he released the crate with our dog still inside it. How long he would have remained in the warehouse cannot be imagined. Baron was finally freed, and we agreed that he should remain in quarantine at our home for at least four weeks before being allowed to go for walks. His crate would be dispatched as soon as possible. We thought it would make a very good kennel.

I always joked about where we might be on the following Christmas. We never seemed to spend any longer than a year in any house, just enough for it to be called home. That year a neighbour asked me to go with her to volunteer as a teacher at the local convent school. I was taken on as an art teacher, and she taught drama. These subjects were not normally in the syllabus for a primary school in New Zealand, so we pioneered these subjects to enlarge the children's imagination. At Christmas the school put on a show, and the children helped paint the backcloth for the scenery for the dramatic Christmas play. I also arranged an exhibition of the children's work at the end-of-year open day. My daughter was now five years old and in the new entrants' class. I taught ten- to thirteen-year-olds in a three-year programme, beginning with the basics of stick figures and ending with ideas about perspective. The head teacher agreed that our contribution had greatly improved the learning capacity of her students.

Once more we moved to an unfurnished chalet high on a cliff's edge overlooking the beach and roaring Pacific Ocean. The sounds of the surf and colony of sandpipers was so great that we could not hear each other in the terraced garden. We had to shut the windows at night; otherwise, we could not sleep. The view looking over the ocean out towards the mountains was magnificent. I joined a pottery class given by the Workers Education Association. Clay was imported from Britain, and the teacher fired the pots in her own kiln. She was very secretive about what glazes she used, and we were not to mix our own.

My husband was headhunted by a building contractor, and I became pregnant. It was thought that if I had another baby, I would feel more settled. New Zealand women were expected to have large families and stay at home to look after the children. I was six months pregnant when some friends down South invited us to spend the holidays with them. The roads outside the towns were made of crushed rock that made driving hazardous, with ruts in the deep levels leaving a trail of dust and shingle billowing out behind. On our way home, the car was lifted up with an enormous thump. As we struck the rock in the middle of the road, I felt the baby in my womb crash down onto my pelvis. In bed that night, I started to bleed, and I prayed that it had not caused a miscarriage.

My doctor had served time in the Islands and was a great believer in letting nature take its course. I was advised to have the end of the bed lifted up at an angle and to remain in bed until the contractions ceased. I was to stay calm and unworried. One of the ladies from the kindergarten said she would take care of our daughter, and I was left alone all day to stay quietly resting. For the first few days, I lay on my side, not daring to move. If I got up, I started to bleed again, but after a while I was able to lie on raised pillows so I could eat and read a book. It was then that I learned to meditate, clearing my mind completely and trusting in the power of God to help me keep the baby full term. My son was expected in March 1962 but was born six weeks earlier. He was put in an incubator, and I was not allowed to feed or see him until a week later.

My husband decided that it might be a good time to buy our own house so that we would feel less transient. We had been dismayed to find that banks were not willing to loan mortgage money as easily as in Britain. In fact, the country was almost bankrupt. Anyone with overseas funds was greatly sought after, especially for obtaining new cars. He found a three-bedroom Summerhill stone house on top of a cliff overlooking the headlands towards the Peninsular. It had been recently built at a reduced price and needed some work done on it. My husband began altering the aspect and configuration of the interior before we moved, in order to separate the living area from the bedrooms.

At the beginning of the Christmas holiday season, I was invited to a morning tea by the boss's wife at their city home. I was told that I could wear a hat if I wanted, but not gloves. I had no idea what kind of social activity this might be but was not prepared for the strange formality of the occasion. We sat demurely around small tables set out on a beautifully manicured lawn, drinking from the very best china cups and saucers. Each cup was from a different tea set with small plates to match. Tea was poured from a silver teapot, and tiny sandwiches, daintily displayed on a cake stand, were handed round. A delicacy named after a famous ballet dancer who had visited New Zealand was served on delicate china plates. Pavlova was a plate-size meringue with a fluffy and fudge-flavoured filling decorated with whipped cream and Chinese gooseberries. Ladies leaned deferentially towards me to ask how I was settling in and from what country I came. I was not like other immigrants they had met, and they found it difficult to recognise my English accent. They imagined life in Britain as something like *Coronation Street* and did not understand I had lived in open countryside before coming to New Zealand.

We did not decorate our house as lavishly at Christmas as we had in England, but we propped the obligatory pine branch in a bucket against the wall. The children were delighted with presents at the staff party, and Father Christmas surprised us by arriving in a helicopter on the beach, throwing toffees into the crowd. We gave dinner parties to our friends and were invited by them to suppers, exchanging gifts and talking until early hours. Our neighbours babysat for us, and we did the same for them.

During the holidays, work colleagues asked if we would like to join them at their seaside house on the Peninsular. They enjoyed waterskiing and fishing, and perhaps we would like to share their barbeque. We had never had a barbeque before and so did not know what to expect. They also had small children, so they could play together with our own family. Upon arriving at the mud and stone beach at the mouth of the harbour, where a motorboat was drawn up, we climbed up onto a grassy knoll, where the children were bouncing around a camp stove. I sat uncomfortably on the side of the hill, slowly slipping downwards, while the wife prepared the meal of lamb chops and salad greens with great hunks of grey bread. The men shot off in the boat while the kids threw mud at each other down at the water's edge.

It was a typical expectation in New Zealand that women stayed behind cooking the meals and caring for the kids while the men played. Soon my husband was dragging himself up on waterskis, and before long was able to stand up and enjoy the experience. I was persuaded to have a go and spent more time under the water than on top. Everyone found it hilarious, but I thought waterskiing overrated. I enjoyed swimming, but being forcibly dragged underwater was not funny. When we got back home, we found we had been badly bitten by sand flies, and the children were covered in itchy spots.

11

Chapter

My Mother arrived from England and stayed with us while my husband helped to build her a house for one just down the road. My sister and her husband arrived later, followed by my husband's parents and married brother. My husband continued to alter our home and make renovations. He was now working for a farming machinery company and borrowed a digger to level our land for a paddle pool and patio. The clay turned to jelly while he was working it, and the digger broke down. Christmas was spent with family and friends, and we holidayed at home. After trying to cook a hot meal for Christmas Day, I realised that it was more sensible to have a cold turkey dinner with salads and summer puddings. We still kept the traditions of Carols by Candlelight and decorating the pine branch. Staff Christmas parties began to wane with economic problems.

In the winter, we went up to the Pass to see the snow and perhaps toboggan on a slope. Suddenly, our car stopped and would not start again. We generally had the dog in the back of the car, but this time he was in the boot. My husband let him out and looked under the bonnet to see why the car was not starting. There was the most awful noise of a dog being run over, and I rushed out of the car to see my beautiful

Gordon Setter underneath a car. We nursed him for two weeks, but he deteriorated and had to be euthanised. I still weep thinking about it.

I immersed myself in various community activities. Parent-teacher meetings at the Convent School were generally chaired by a man. It was believed that women were not able to run a meeting properly and were only capable of making tea. This attitude ran through the whole of New Zealand society, so when it came to elect a new Chairperson and no male offered his name, I volunteered. I became the very first female Chairperson for the school PTA. I helped to start a pottery group in a disused electricity substation, where we put an electric kiln. We went out on field trips to dig clay and experimented with refining it and making glazes. We bought electric driven pottery wheels and invited experts from overseas to give us hints for making ceramics. I also obtained a licence to work a cinema projector so that I could get films from the National Library and show them to the Pottery Association and the Parents' Association.

One morning as I was bathing my son and looking out of the kitchen window at the calm sea and the jagged headlands, I was transfixed to the spot by a tremendous surge of energy. The hairs on my arms lifted because it seemed that I was being bathed in light. I babbled like a baby, and everything was made clear. I wrote poetry, painted pictures, and joined various art groups. I wrote a story for my neighbour's daughter and illustrated it. It was a sudden and dramatic occurrence that would eventually change my life later. I began questioning everything. Was all the teaching I had been given true? Who was I? The person inside me did not fit the glove I was wearing. I felt as if I was at the bottom of a swimming pool, struggling to get to the top. I discovered that this numinous experience had been shared by several people around the world.

My second son was born in October 1964. My mother's sister and husband came over to visit, and we held a large christening party in our garden near to Christmas. I had a bad prolapse because he had been born forehead first and got stuck, so I needed major uplift surgery. Through connections he had made in the industry, my husband was offered a Sales Manager job for a cement company. We were nicely settled, and the garden was flourishing. My daughter was taking riding lessons, and we had good friendly neighbours. We were just starting to enjoy our achievements.

My husband decided to sell the house, and it sold very quickly. Suddenly we were homeless. I found a one-bedroom, furnished cliffside cabin for rent overlooking the estuary. The boys had their beds in the sunroom at the entrance, and my daughter had her bed in the sitting room. Our bedroom and bathroom were off the kitchen, so the children had to walk through to use the bathroom. The interior of the cabin had been designed by a well-known early architect, with wood panels and a river stone fireplace. It was perfect for a Christmas atmosphere. Although it was cramped, it was probably the happiest time we had ever had anywhere because of the holiday atmosphere.

My daughter started High School, and my first son began school at the Convent. We had one cat called Boots, and he enjoyed clambering and hunting around the bush covered cliffside. Salt bush, aloes, and pride of Madeira abounded in a flush of luxuriant colour, along with pelargoniums and ice plant. I had never seen such a wonderful display. One day while walking up the steep path with my shopping, I heard a kitten mewing in a bush. She followed me up to the cabin, but I did not let her in. The next day, she was still sitting outside. She soon became part of our family.

December brought with it North-west winds that blew straight from the Southern Alps in a sizzling heat. Everything wilted, and the tar roads melted. We ate our Christmas dinner overlooking the sandy beach from our cliffside garden. New friends were made with my husband's colleagues, and I went with one of the wives to choose the children's Christmas gifts for the staff party. It was great fun selecting the toys, and we became very good friends with them, visiting their holiday home in one of the bays on the Peninsular. At their beach, we went diving into the surf to collect huge kelp fronds to make bags to wrap around mussels that were scraped from the rocks. The mussels were steamed in a kelp bag on a campfire, and we ate them straight from the open shells. We had never had toasted sandwiches before, and they showed us how to make them. Slices of bread were buttered on each side, then stuffed with tomatoes and cheese, and fried on both sides until golden brown.

At that time in the sixties and seventies, life was very basic with very little contact outside of the country. There were few restaurants in town, and cafes only sold hot pies. People entertained at home, giving large dinner parties at Christmas and during the holiday season. Recipes such as beef stroganoff and veal fillet were popular. Casseroles were very new. Most people bought sides of lamb from the freezing works, and roast was always on the menu. People ate lamb chops or steak for breakfast with mussels or battered paua and oyster patties. I had never seen so much meat eaten in one day, every day.

12
Chapter

Christmas was a time of plenty, with housewives busy bottling and preserving fruit and vegetables grown in gardens or bought in boxes from a local fruit farm. There were exotic vegetables that we had never come across before. Kumara and sweet potato, green plantains, aubergines and asparagus—these were luxuries in Britain but were common in the Chinese green grocers. There were Chinese gooseberries (now known as kiwifruit), tamarillo (which was called tree tomato), boysenberries, persimmons, pear and apple quince, and pawpaw. We grew banana passion fruit on our boundary Ngaio trees, and we ate the succulent seeds with a spoon. My husband was told he could pick as many cherry plums in a colleague's garden as he could carry; they would ripen in the middle of their holiday away and rot on the ground. I made jars of jam that lasted until the following season. We regularly went to the apricot fruit farm down a valley close to home and came back laden with large boxes of almost ripe golden fruit. I bottled most of it, and we ate the rest as it ripened.

We had a small circle of business friends, and I made contacts through the children's schools. I joined the various city art clubs and presented my paintings for exhibition in town art galleries. I also gained my driving licence, and my husband bought me a vintage car for Christmas. There were very few modern cars on the roads apart from the Australian Holden that had enough room in the back for a hoard of children. I joked that Britain had shooting brakes for all their dogs, but New Zealanders had wagons for all their kids.

After coming home from a trip around the north of the South Island, we found a holiday cottage for rent in one of the sounds. Previously we had enjoyed a wonderful holiday in a small complex that was only accessible by boat. It had been infested with wasps that ate the fish we caught on the jetty, and one of the children was stung. The cottage was ideal and just across the sound to the Outward Bound School. The water was wonderfully warm, clear, and full of fish. My husband hired a small boat with an outboard motor, and we explored the coves and marvelled at the tree ferns and thick bush that came down to the water's edge. We stayed at the cottage every year for the Christmas break until the owner died and the house was renovated by the new owner. It somehow lost its ambience.

My husband always put a lot of effort into our holidays in the sounds, hiring motor launches so we could explore the waterways. I enjoyed helping to haul the boat onto a trailer and launching it at the turn of tide. I did not appreciate the importance of catching the tides at odd times of the day and possibly having to coordinate disgruntled kids and meal times to fit in with the schedule. At one time, we were in the middle of a wide piece of water when the engine stopped and refused to start. A squall suddenly appeared, whipping the water up and threatening to tip the boat. We managed to use some paddles to take us to the shore and dragged the boat up to a small jetty. We were shipwrecked. There were one or two holiday homes on shore, and fortunately a man who had been watching our distress through binoculars called the milk boat to pick us up. We were towed to safety, calling around the coves to deliver mail and milk and collect a couple of ewes.

After a while, my husband started to look for a suitable plot of land on which to build a house. He engaged a young architect and a builder, and between them they designed a sturdy, two-storey home on the lower slopes of a local hill. The two sitting rooms, kitchen diner, and entrance were at road level, and the four bedrooms, en-suite, family bathroom, and utility room were downstairs. The upstairs ceilings had exposed beams, rafters, and sarking, with a rough-faced brown brick chimney and fireplace in the sitting room. Floor-to-ceiling windows were on each floor with double-layer concrete block walls. There was a veranda along the front facing the sea towards the mountains, and wood decks were built outside each bedroom.

It took several months to finish the build, and my husband said he would do the interior work so we could move in. Walls had to be painted, doors put on the wardrobes, carpet had to be put down, and floor boards had to be treated. I sewed curtain material bought from a local store for our bedroom and the sitting rooms. We sat on deck chairs and an old settee suite that I'd recovered. My husband made a dining table out of an old door; it rocked when carving meat. We found a set of coronation chairs at a sale. I designed and planted the hillside back garden and obtained a gardener to create a Japanese style garden in the front. Most of the Christmas break and every weekend was spent working on the house.

13

Several social and family events occurred during the seventies and eighties that were to radically alter our lives. New Zealand had always been a Socialist country with a pioneering population. The economy relied solely on agriculture and had benefited from supplying the American troops in the Pacific. The European Trade Agreement had decreased New Zealand exports to Britain, President Kennedy had been assassinated, and Russia had given up the Mao form of communism in favour of socialist capitalism. Because of the Vietnam War, underground communism was creeping into our schools in the form of *Chairman Mao's Little Red Handbook*. Any authority given by parents and the ruling classes should be questioned and ignored. Young people went on Stop the Vietnam War marches and rallies.

A local Psychiatrist, concerned about the lack of healthy interests for teenagers, developed an environmental club called Exploraction, and I was appointed Secretary. We held meetings at a local high school, inviting other schools to join us. It was my job to research and provide professional people from the University to give talks about their favourite subjects and take us on field trips. Many of the lecturers had interesting hobbies like astronomy, marine biology, and archaeology. We even had a person from a UFO study group come to lecture. The Psychiatrist was also a botanist, and we went into the bush to learn about native plants and trees. At Christmas, we took the group to a Marine Biology Centre farther up the coast and studied the creatures on the shoreline. The area was special because the deep waters caused by a rift between the mountains and sea floor created an upwelling of deep sea life.

My husband's company was expanding, and the shareholding became international. He was promoted and put in charge of moving the company to another site and helping to design new offices. For the Christmas holidays, we rented a small cottage in the harbour across the water from the port. I wondered why it was that we seemed to have such a lot of spare time while on holiday that we did not have at home. The place was furnished with old Edwardian chairs beside a log fire and very basic bedrooms and kitchen. My husband looked at the possibility of buying a holiday house somewhere on the Peninsular, and we looked at various locations around the harbour and on the far side of the peninsular. Most of them had no sewers or fresh water supplies. Rainwater was collected from the roof and stored in tanks, and sewage drained out into the harbour.

At the time, I was suffering from a terrible backache at the bottom of my spine. I had been taking hormone replacement therapy after my previous operation. I woke one morning to find I had been bleeding heavily in the night. My doctor immediately made an appointment with a specialist, who discovered I had enormous fibroids in my womb. The surgery was not made easy by my previous uplift operation, and the extraction was very difficult. I bled a lot, and apparently my heart stopped. I had a near-death experience during which, as if looking from above, I could see the surgical crew trying to revive me.

At Christmas that year, we looked after a small cabin for a woman and her husband in a gorge. They wanted us to look after their sheep by opening gates into new pastures every few days. We had to feed their old dog and a pet wild pig. Piggy was a real character who loved swimming in the river, and our youngest son rode on his back in the water. We bathed naked in the gushing stream and surfed the waterfalls down into a deep swirling pool. Robin, our English Setter, sat in a canoe and looked surprised as he drifted round and round in the pool. Those were happy days, full of sun and laughter. We picnicked on the stony beach. and I sketched the river and boulders with the bush reflected in the water.

We stayed at the cabin several times, and once it snowed when we were there. I had cooked the turkey on Christmas Eve and wrapped it in tinfoil and brown baking paper for the journey up to the gorge. My daughter and her girl friend were to earn money picking fruit in a nearby orchard, but the weather was so wet the fruit rotted before it could be picked. It was incredibly cold in the cabin, and the turkey was soggy and tasteless. Piggy had been killed by a local farmer who was frightened that a wild pig might get in with his purebred pigs. The dog had died of old age, and the sheep were sold to the neighbouring farmer. The woman and her family had become good friends, so we were intrigued to find they were building a large house farther down the valley. We were invited to stay when it was completed.

14
Chapter

My sister and her husband lived in a house they had built on a section under a prominent cliff. They had two girls, and our children often played with them. The eldest girl was about the same age as our youngest boy, and they got along very well. My sister gave a party for everyone at Christmas and invited our mother and other friends as well. Japanese students occasionally lodged with them. My sister provided a great feast at Christmas, with her husband cooking his favourite steak teriyaki and my sister providing coq au vin. The table was filled with vegetable dishes and fruits, nuts and dried fruits. Sometimes we ate at the table or took a plateful out into the garden. A large, beautifully decorated pine branch stood in the corner of the room with daintily wrapped parcels hidden among the branches. As the cousins grew older, they found these gatherings boring and longed to escape with their friends. The Jehovah Witnesses called on her one day and told her that this was a pagan ritual. One day, she declared she was never going to celebrate Christmas again and would concentrate on the holiday season instead. From then on, she did not give presents or any special parties. Instead, we gave each other un-Christmas presents at different times of the year.

We toured the North Island for a once-in-a-lifetime trip. My daughter spent most of the time swatting for exams. The eldest son had croup brought on by the smoke from the volcanic vents in Rotorua, and the youngest got bitten badly by sandflies. My husband brooded moodily, apparently worried by the loss of time at work. It was the last family holiday we all enjoyed together.

My mother began to holiday, with my sister and family, at a thermal Springs during the holidays. We visited for the day and gloried in the thermal pools and deciduous European forest planted around a Victorian rehabilitation hospital. At that time, concrete plunge pools were built inside the hospital and were gender separated. We bathed naked and were careful not to scrape ourselves on the concrete sides in case we became infected with irritable welts. There were no changing rooms, so we undressed and dressed beside the old-fashioned radiators in the hospital corridor leading to the pools. My sister always provided a roast beef dinner afterwards, and we returned home by car, leaving them behind at their motel.

My husband suggested I do a Liberal Studies course at the local University. It was three years of intensive study, at the end of which was a Certificate and points towards a Degree. I was in my element studying Metaphysics, Comparative Religions, Introduction to Human Development, Genetics, and Ecology. I passed the course in two years. Around the same period, the Women's Movement was beginning to emerge in Australia, and my sister and I were co-opted to do a survey of New Zealand women. Very little was known about their education standards and aspirations. Most women had no education beyond Primary school; their aspirations did not go beyond marriage and children. A few were given a hairdressing business or became teachers and nurses. Women were regarded as second-class citizens. I gave a keynote speech at the Inaugural meeting of Women's Liberation in New Zealand, and a big Conference was organised in the auditorium of the town hall. Only women were invited, and men were banned, which caused a problem with journalists covering the event.

The Conference lasted three days over a long weekend, and I joined a group watching an alternative religious ceremony performed. It turned out to be a form of Wicca, with a priestess enacting the Gaia ritual without the male counterpart. The fallout from attending a pagan ritual can only be imagined. The fact that we were having an all-women conference was also thought very radical, as was women claiming the right to have a voice. Women's clubs sprang up all over town, with places pronounced 'Women Only'. It was pleasant to call in for a glass of wine without being accosted by a male making sexual insinuations. Women began reading books by an Australian woman and other female authors; *The Women's Room* and *The Female Eunuch* were popular reading. Women started to apply for male jobs, insisting that females be introduced into all-male clubs and schools, and they generally challenged the patriarchal society in New Zealand.

Eventually, the whole movement was taken over by a group of prominent lesbians. They formed collectives and gave art exhibitions. Great emphasis was put on female genitals and acceptance by society. Menstruation and the womb were favourite subjects for artistic expression. A torn wedding dress placed on the floor, and enormous sanitary pads hung at the entrance to art exhibitions, set the scene. At Christmas, I was invited to take part in a Female Collective art exhibition. I had been painting a series on the Apollo moon landing, showing the torso of a male dancer against a collage of the moon and earth. It was placed behind a large pot plant in the gallery. I also gave a recital of my poetry to a female writers' group that was well received.

My husband decided to build a sailing dinghy and encouraged us all to sail in her on the estuary. None of us knew the first thing about sailing, and usually we ended upside down after endeavouring to tack across the water. The boys were not enamoured with being dunked in cold water and feared drowning. The fact that it was possible to stand up on the mud at the bottom of the lagoon was no incentive.

15
Chapter

One day I noticed a lump growing in my throat just under the Adam's apple. I had difficulty in swallowing, and the lump felt sore. I was sent to an endocrinologist, who was very concerned it might be cancerous. He sent me for a radiology scan in Christchurch Hospital, which showed a tulip-like tumour in my gullet attached to my thyroid. The very delicate surgery was a success, and I returned home feeling pleased with life. Our home looked inviting and comfortable, and our family was growing up. My husband had become a successful businessman, and I felt I could finally enjoy the comforts we had worked towards.

By 1977, I had moved to a single-storey Summerhill-stone house in a seaside suburb with my children and my English Setter dog. My daughter, now twenty-one, was partly living at home and partly in a student flat. She attended Teachers College. My eldest son, now fifteen, had finally passed his driving test and was learning to ride a motorbike. The youngest son was thirteen and had just started High School. As part of divorce proceedings, my Volkswagen car was sold and, I bought a small second-hand Ford, which we loaded up with a canoe and suitcases for our Christmas holiday at the gorge. Our English setter sat regally in the back with my youngest son, and my eldest son drove the whole way. We arrived at the cabin in good time, with instructions to use the freezer contents. I was overwhelmed at such generosity. There were several goats to look after that clambered over the car, and my sons soon took charge of the farm quad bikes. Halfway through our stay, my friend came home and provided us with a feast, introducing many of her Bohemian friends. After dinner, we all bathed naked in the gorge, enjoying the sensual, cool water on exposed skin. It was total freedom without a hint of sexuality.

My sister persuaded me to join a singles club in town to widen my social horizon. I was very naïve and unworldly because my husband was the only man I had known intimately. I was totally unprepared for the expectations of this group of fringe people. I had to lose many inhibitions and struggled for a long while with the concept of free love. I became a hippie, joined a group of New Life Christians, was baptised, and decided to continue with my University studies. Although throughout my life I have met some wonderful people and learned a lot from them, I have never wanted to live with anyone else. I reasoned that marriage was a one-time commitment.

I tie-dyed the boys' bedroom curtains and hung others taken from the old house. I kept most of the furniture. The boys quickly made new friends and annoyed the neighbours by skateboarding down the drive. Someone gave me a gramophone, and we bought our first vinyl album. We had a small pool table, and soon the living room was full of large teenage boys enjoying themselves. We had lots of late-night parties as they grew older, with friends coming and going at all hours. The house was always full of loud music and dancing. Happily, I was asked to join in, as well as provide burgers and hot dogs.

Many of the young people who visited my home were from broken marriages. In fact, it was unusual to find people who were in their first marriages. It seemed that because of the female emancipation that had occurred and the advent of the Pill, there was far less tolerance of male behaviour. Male supremacy was no longer acceptable. I often sat in on long discussions about how they coped with what was happening, and they used the psychology books in my library and self-help manuals. I encouraged some of my sons' friends to have legitimate sessions of breaking old plates and throwing tantrums. We all needed therapy to release tension and a way of vandalising without causing harm. One of the spontaneous games we had was eating a banana and throwing the skins at each other. It always ended up with raucous laughter, screaming, and the brown skin splitting into pieces and splattering on the walls. I used to find old pieces of banana skin behind furniture weeks later and smudges on the old wallpaper that never got cleaned.

16
Chapter

As a divorced woman, I found I did not receive many invitations to dinner with old friends. There were coffee mornings with women friends, but even they became fewer as time went on. Couples were considered more acceptable. I found myself on my own most of the time, with family preferring to be with friends of their own age. I found a Saturday job for my eldest son, sweeping a wood toy factory floor. At College he had excelled in Accounting, and the owner asked him to keep the books for him. My younger son was studying for School Certificate, and my daughter had finished Teachers College and was in her first year teaching at a local school.

We went up to my friend's new place in the gorge and used the time to have a look at various communes. I had the notion that perhaps we could form a commune of our own. There were various kinds, some of which were rather basic and badly run. Others were based on the kibbutz style of Socialist sharing, with no one owning any property and earnings distributed evenly between the members. It was interesting that the gender divisions were still maintained, with women looking after children and men doing outside work. When we returned home, I discovered I already had a commune with all the kids sleeping on the floor and using the food in the refrigerator. I rather fancied having an old railway carriage in the backyard or a gypsy caravan in a field somewhere. Perhaps I'd keep bees and become vegetarian. One day my singles club friend asked if I would accompany him to a Christian rally at the Town Hall. I was totally spiritually awakened, and from then on, all kinds of amazing and synchronistic events occurred that changed my outlook on life.

I received an unsolicited newsletter from a Benedictine Abbot. He described a trip he had made to a Japanese botanic garden where a sensitive bush grew. When touched, the leaves curled up, and it took a long while before they unfurled. He had taken this metaphor as a spiritual message. Aloneness was not some kind of punishment but a gift from God. It took a short time to be hurt, but it took a long while to heal. I thought it was all very well because he had chosen his solitary lifestyle, whereas mine had been bestowed on me. I had never before had a choice to make my own decisions. I had to ask before I did or thought anything. After a while, I realised it was true. Solitariness is a gift for mindfulness and review, for non-thinking and just being, for just staring at the sky through a canopy of leaves.

One Christmas, my friend wrote that a pen friend of hers from overseas was coming over, and she wanted to go to the city cathedral. She said that something had urged her to be there at Christmas. One of the sides of the volcano rose up behind my house. Someone had planted a coppice of pine trees on the steep cliffside, and I had grubbed out some steps leading up to a sun deck. The boys had helped to build the deck cantilevered out from the hillside, and we often sunbathed in deck chairs or drank gin and tonic while watching satellites sailing across the sky. The American lady had been with an Indian tribe learning shaman rituals, and she was so taken with my deck and the ambience of it that she insisted on having a smudging ritual in my honour. The significance of this was not known until much later, but I had not gone to visit the Indian tribe—they had come to visit me. After the ritual of sacred stones and feathers and gongs, she wafted some smoke towards my face and scraped at my chest with an eagle feather, throwing whatever it was she had released over her shoulder and up into the sky. I felt an extraordinary sense of calm and restoration. I no longer wandered around the hill thinking there was nothing. I now knew that I am.

I looked at the walnut tree that hung over the next-door fence, and I marvelled at how long it must have been there. The cottage behind looked at least a hundred years old, so it had probably been planted then. Walnuts are not native New Zealand trees. The nut might have come on one of the first colonising ships, or it might have been dropped from a Christmas parcel sent from France. As I looked at the tree, I thought of the wonderful strength and resilience of that tree and the stresses and strains it must have experienced. Yet here it was, still flowering and bearing fruit. Then I thought of the forests of trees that had ever lived and those still living, and the power of their survival in spite of climate changes. How remarkable and flexible they were. If I could use all that energy and power in myself, then I could do anything. I thought God must be like this, powerful and flexible like a tree.

Christmas has always been family time, and I had always enjoyed the lead-up to it, choosing presents for overseas parcels and sending cards to distant relatives and friends. I still wrote to my brother, who had emigrated to South Africa about the same time as we had gone to New Zealand. He lived in a smart bungalow in a suburb of Johannesburg. He wrote in his Christmas message that he had colon cancer, and he described the hilarious experiences he had trying to hold a conference with his colonoscopy bag farting every few minutes. He was on the way to recovery but still may not survive the cancer. I decided to visit him.

My daughter had finished her primary school term, and she and a friend had toured the islands as a preamble for her overseas trip to Europe. My sons were busy enjoying their own lifestyles. The eldest was a youth leader, taking young people camping in the bush and mountains. The youngest went surfing and skiing with his motorbike club. Both of them played squash and tennis at the local courts with their father.

17

Chapter

In 1981, the South African rugby team was about to tour Britain. There was a large radical movement in New Zealand and Australia against apartheid, and they organised riots to stop the matches from taking place. Air traffic between the countries was stopped due to strikes by the crews, and my booking was affected. I managed to travel with Air New Zealand to Australia, and the flight was cancelled to Johannesburg. I was stranded in Sydney for three days until a flight was secretly arranged on a foreign plane, and we left under cover of darkness. My brother met me at the airport and introduced me to his male partner and a Zimbabwean manservant.

I was taken by my brother on a tour of the country in his Mercedes car, which I drove some of the time. We visited a museum, where I studied their collection of hominid skulls and the history of elephants. They were experimenting with crossing lions with tigers and donkeys with zebras. The offspring were infertile. I noted that wild animals caged were the same as humans caged in their tiny dwellings. Humans had been domesticated as well and suffered just as much from isolation as other animals. I wrote an essay on the subject and sent it back to my Human Development tutor at the Extramural establishment where I was enrolled for an Arts Degree. We went to the diamond mines and then to the Boer War prisoner encampment, where women and children had starved to death. We went to a famous town and watched the black South African surf team training on the beach. We went up in the funicular to the top of a mountain and ate the best chocolate cake I had ever had. We gloried at the wild flowers along the cliffs beyond and were saddened by the demise of the elephants and beach leopards in the area.

We saw the ramshackle African temporary village about which the Western media was always concerned. It was a collection of cardboard and tin huts that were occasionally pulled down, and residents were checked for entry visas. If they could speak English or Afrikaans and had work permits, they could remain; otherwise, they were sent to Home Territories. An employment tax was paid by the South Africans to the parent country for every employed person. Employing someone without a permit was an offence. African nationals had special privileges, free transport, education, and medication. Some of the poorest people were aged whites and European settlers.

We stayed in rondovals and smart Company flats, and in a charming hotel where we climbed a high mountain; I dug up a fossilised dinosaur toe. We scrambled through holes and up chimneys in a wondrous cave gallery, where a symphony concert had once been staged, and we wallowed in thermal pools where the mineral water sparkled inside our bathing costumes. Up the coast, I slid down a huge water slide and watched a native dance in a traditional village. When it finished, the African owner changed his costume and drove off in his Mercedes car. We went to see the native dancing at the gold mines, and I bought a piece of mounted rock containing a seam of gold.

We went on a wilderness safari in the Northern territories. I had imagined a nice tourist location overlooking a safari park, but this was a wild camping trip. We had basic camp beds and outdoor washing facilities, a hole in the ground as a toilet, and a bucket with holes in it for showering. We had to be careful of snakes hiding in the loo. A campfire alight all the time was constantly stacked with fresh fuel, and we were expected to make our own basic food consisting of ground mealie meal and sardine salads. We had encounters with lions whilst trekking and close shaves with wild pigs and hyenas. Wildebeest, giraffe, zebra were plentiful, but crashing around in the Company four-wheeler certainly discouraged elephants and lions. I was surprised by a hedgehog in our tent one night and realised that most animals obviously originated in Africa. We went out on tramps into the veldt every day, and the grasses and ticks screwed their way into our clothing, causing nasty sores. I cried when I got back to my brother's house, relieved to be back in civilisation.

Upon my return to New Zealand, the local newspaper that had wanted me to smuggle out copy would only print negative stories about the plight of the Africans and refused to accept that their education system was the same as ours. They did not believe that they had the largest Government State Housing in the world or that many Africans there lived in luxury houses with servants of their own.

After my South African trip, I took a six-month job working as a Census Analyst to pay off a loan. When that expired, I applied to be a Field Officer, finding jobs for students. I had stood in an unemployment queue for years, and at my age it was difficult to find permanent jobs. Most of these were subsidised by the Government for six months to solve the unemployment problem. Working at the education establishment was ideal because I had access to the library and could take my term examinations there. I found my youngest son a job at a hospitality place near the airport, where he became an odd-job man. I gave a huge party on Christmas Eve, picnicking on the new lower deck built by my youngest son. We feasted on ham salad, pavlova, and fruit salad with lashings of ice cream.

I had decided long ago that our winter ritual of Father Christmas, holly and mistletoe, and fake snow was inappropriate in midsummer when people went on holiday. Instead, we should celebrate it as Summer Solstice and have Christmas dinner in the middle of winter. Winter was cold, with icy winds blowing from the South Pole onto the Southern Alps. It brought snow and hard frosts that lingered under clear, sunny skies. Winter Solstice was the shortest day of the year. I decorated the house with fir branches cut from the pines on my cliffside. Invitations were sent to friends, relatives, and a few neighbours. I cooked a variety of dishes, including slumgullion, which is a slow-cooked beef stew with lots of vegetables, pulses, grains, spices, herbs, and sultanas. It is left to stew for at least twenty-four hours and then allowed to cool. Then it's reheated when desired next day. The party was a great success, and as everyone left, I handed out token presents to each guest. My youngest son introduced the idea of a mid-winter feast to the hospitality establishment where he worked, and it became an annual tradition complete with Father Christmas.

18

Chapter

This period in my life was a series of confused events that produced great spiritual insights on one hand and total frustration on the other. My daughter had returned to Britain on an overseas trip and, had met a young man through my cousins' acquaintances in Surrey. She had thought of a quick visit home, but I decided to visit her instead. My daughter was sharing a lovely country house with three girls and was teaching new entrants at a local private school. It was the first time I had returned to my homeland, and it was more emotionally charged than I had imagined. My daughter took me on an exploratory trip to all the places I remembered, as well as others that I had never been to before. We went up North to see our home and went to the West Country to explore and visit old friends. The countryside was more beautiful and lush than I remembered it, and I returned to New Zealand revitalised. I determined to return in two years.

This was to set a pattern created by a curious need to live overseas far away from family ties, yet I still longed for the comfort and closeness they brought. On one of my visits, we made a quick trip across the Channel to a hypermarket in France to obtain a carload of cheap wine. Another time, I took the ferry across to Boulogne and then the night train to the South, where my daughter and her boyfriend met me. We camped in a vineyard, ate croissants with marmalade, and drank champagne on the beach. I sunbathed topless, much to the amazement of the boyfriend. It was on my return home that they announced their engagement with a country-style wedding next summer. They came back to New Zealand for a marriage blessing ceremony to include all the family in the celebrations.

My eldest son had met a lovely girl and become engaged, with a wedding planned soon after. The youngest son decided to represent his father at my daughter's wedding and give her away. With all the confusion, I suddenly found myself sitting on my sundeck totally on my own with my beautiful English Setter and my cats. I decided to join a group of people seeking Universal Truths. My drama friend opened her home to the group, and we met to study and debate the findings of various religious and cosmology authors and philosophers.

A vicar and his wife were examining the phenomenon of synchronicity, and I took part in their discussions. I began to experience synchronistic events, especially concerning windows. Semiconscious and recovering from gall bladder surgery, I had seen someone who looked like a friend knocking on the ward window. Impossibly, I opened the window to see my mother's sister outside, dressed in green. She said she had come to say farewell but could not stay. When I returned home, my cousin phoned to say that my aunt had died in England at exactly the time she'd visited me. From previous experience, I learned that the window was significant in understanding the electromagnetic energy that divided spirit from material events. If the window was opened, full potential possibilities were revealed; they were limitless. What was heard, seen, and felt behind a closed window was nothing compared with the expanded landscape of an open window.

Through the Seekers Group, I attended a series of lectures. A person from overseas came to chat with me in the group library. He handed me one of the books, saying that I should study it. I never saw him again. It was the opening to yet more synchronistic events that resulted in my giving workshops and lectures on the Essene Gospel of Peace and on the Universal Tree of Life. I used motivational and inspirational workshops on spiritual development and a guide to creative mindfulness as teaching tools. I was invited to lecture on various subjects, introducing brain therapies for simultaneous development of both hemispheres and meditation techniques. I dressed up as a wise woman wearing a fox fur, a shawl with tassels, and a mandala pendant to lecture about Odin and the Scandinavian runes. It was an exciting time.

My eldest son came home one day saying that his Company was being wound down. Through my contacts with working on the Student Jobs team, I arranged for a loan to buy the Company. Each initial member had to buy an equal amount of shares and have equal voting rights. I bought a shareholding, and when my job ended, I worked on the wood planing machine in the factory. The company flourished, but after a while I could not keep pace with demand in the production line. Christmas was always a good time for a factory party. One or two of the workers played in a band and provided entertainment. I have always enjoyed freestyle and ballroom dancing, so I let my hair down and joined in.

My eldest son's wife and my daughter were expecting babies. I decided to spend Christmas in England now that my daughter was settled in a house in Surrey. Her husband ran a catering business and would be busy at Christmas. I thought she would need help while she looked after the baby. I felt I should have been there when the baby was born. The feeling was so strong that I felt an intense need to go.

19
Chapter

Besides running a successful business, my son-in-law was renovating their Edwardian terrace house. The nursery was the only room completed. I shared it with my baby granddaughter. My daughter spent most of her time caring for her baby in the comfort of this bedroom. Bathing and breastfeeding took a great deal of the morning. As it was nearing the season of Company dinners, there were large bags of potatoes and Brussels sprouts to be prepared. Turkeys rested in the refrigerator, ingredients for the stuffing were prepared separately, and tiny sausages wrapped in bacon and a variety of vegetables were ready to be cooked. Individual Christmas puddings stored in the freezer were thawing on the kitchen shelf. There were mountains of washing up—pans to be scoured and utensils to be polished soaked in the small kitchen sink. Old, forgotten cups of coffee and tea littered any surface not covered with food preparation. It seemed I was destined to bring some order to this chaos.

My daughter was anxious to show me all the wonders of pre-Christmas events. The country town was resplendent with brightly coloured decorations, sparkling store fronts with animated figures, and a marketplace brimming with holly, ivy, and mistletoe. There were stalls selling large Norway spruce trees and colourful berry wreaths. The butcher shop was festooned with braces of pheasant and turkeys hung on spikes outside the shop. Christmas music rang out of every store. The place bustled with energy. For a special treat, we went with my son-in-law's family to watch a fireworks display and torchlight parade at a nearby village. The baby was carried in a bag strapped to her father's front while we wrapped ourselves in warm coats, scarves, and beanie hats. An even more exciting event took us into London to marvel at the lights, the store windows, and the enormous spruce tree donated annually by Norway.

The front room was in the process of being renovated, with plaster dust everywhere. The fireplace that had been covered over by a modern tiled unit had now been restored with a Victorian iron and tile hearth. My daughter hoped I would help her decorate the tree and that we would make it into a shared and special event. I was overwhelmed and very emotional, and I tried to not show how I felt so as not to spoil the experience. In the middle of all the preparations, the washing machine decided to leak onto the kitchen floor. On Christmas Eve, we went to midnight service at the village church, and on Boxing Day I stayed with my son, who was living over a service station in a nearby village. While looking out of the bedroom window, I was surprised to see a man digging in his garden. Winter did not appear to be as severe as it used to be because roses, fuchsias, and dahlias were still in flower. We wrapped ourselves in our duvets and watched animated films on television. We climbed up a prominent wooded hill and looked out across the countryside to the beacon on the top of a distant hill towards the coast. The view was magnificent. We talked in-depth about our lives and what my son hoped to achieve.

Men played golf even on Christmas Day. I often walked alongside the course with my daughter's black Labrador, with the trees dripping with thawing frost. It was a favourite haunt for dog walkers. The track took us deep within a wood that in later years would be flattened by a hurricane. There was a special oak tree where my daughter often sat to meditate, and I made a sketch of it for her as a remembrance of my visit. Soon it was time to leave, and I decided to return for my granddaughter's first birthday in September the following year.

20

I managed to visit my family in England every two or three years. I grew familiar with the different airlines offering cheap flights that took me to various airports. From New Zealand, it was necessary to fly on Air New Zealand. At that time, the local airport runway could not accommodate long-haul airplanes. Up North, there was a long walk from the interior airport to the overseas one, along a narrow open walkway alongside the runways. It was necessary to check in and go through security procedures, although they were not nearly as restrictive as they are now.

The Australian 707 planes were spacious, and the crew was eager to assist. I generally obtained a seat by the window so that I could rest my head on the bulwark and gaze at the view of the ground slowly slipping past and the wonderful cloud formations beneath. In contrast, the Oriental Airlines crew were tightly controlling, refusing to allow anyone to look out of the windows while the overhead film screen was operating. Japanese airlines were a delightful experience with numerous servings of green tea to calm the nerves. During an obligatory stopover, small rooms filtering calming and meditative music were provided in a hotel, along with slippers and a happi coat laid out on the bed.

While on these trips, I took advantage of visiting other places. I attended Body, Mind, and Spirit Conferences and festivals. I met interesting people, and learned new things. My youngest son lived in a hotel in the South of France as an Agent, going to the station to pick up backpackers looking for accommodation. I was invited by the hoteliers to come over for a couple of weeks as their guest. I was expected to prepare the breakfast tables; help put out the french bread, soft cheese, and jam spread; serve the very thick coffee; and clear up afterwards. I worked the ironing rollers pressing pillowcases and sheets at the entrance to the café, greeting visitors with a cheery French phrase as they passed. During the afternoons, my son and I explored the surrounding hilltop villages. We explored right into the backcountry, home of the perfumeries, and marvelled at the grandeur of the French Alps where eagles flew.

On one occasion, my drama friend accompanied me to visit my cousin in Canada, where we were taken to Niagara Falls and explored the shores of a beautiful lake. She had friends on the West Coast, and her friends showed us some interesting areas in town. We were very impressed with the Art Nouveau and Art Deco architecture in the city. One of her friends lived on a houseboat on the river. It was beautifully decorated, and a lovely potted garden graced the deck. The ladies cooked a turkey in our honour, and a Jewish friend wrote a wonderful and moving prayer for me. I felt so emotional that I cried. It was as if I had discovered my soul tribe.

Whilst in London, I stayed at a Benedictine Retreat Centre for a few days. I had wanted to meet a Brother from Canada who was staying there and finishing off a book he was writing. I missed him by a couple of days, however it gave me a chance to explore and go into places where my grandparents had shopped. Such luxury was overwhelming, especially contrasting with what was available at that time in New Zealand. The food halls were lavish and assortment of fine china was incredible. The Christmas shop was a fairy land with life-size toys and glittering decorated trees. I walked through the parks and gardens all the way to the river without seeing a single car. I went down below ground into a beautifully clean, world-famous women's toilet with vases of flowers on the vanity shelves.

The Sisters who ran the Benedictine Retreat House took us to a service at the Russian Orthodox church. People stood around in the centre of the building or sat on benches against the walls. Russian music seemed to be broadcast from the roof, with deep bass rumblings and chanting. A closed screen in front of the altar suddenly opened, a bearded man with staring eyes peered through and uttered something, and the screen closed again. People passed around little rice cakes, and a veiled woman collected the dripping candle wax from the lights burning in front of various gilded icons. While looking around the congregation, I was surprised to see a well-known kung fu actor, but then I thought I was there, so why should it be a surprise to see him there too? After the service that seemed never-ending, we were introduced to the Archbishop, who pronounced a benediction over us and then made a prophecy to me. I cannot remember what it was now, but it was very significant at the time.

Various people came to visit me in New Zealand. Friends whom I stayed with in their beautiful thatched cottage came to stay with me during a tour of New Zealand. I took them on a boat trip to see the dolphins in the volcanic harbour on the other side of the Peninsular. A Canadian couple and their large son, who I met while visiting my son in France, also stayed with me. They were teachers, and they worked for half a year and then spent the next six months travelling around the world. My youngest son met a Scottish girl while skiing. She applied for a job in New Zealand for a two-year contract, and they invited me up to stay for Christmas. Her parents came over from Scotland, and we were entertained with a sumptuous Christmas dinner on a farm in the backcountry. After a lively horse ride around the tree fern bush and admiring the farmer's new pig dog pups, my son announced their engagement. I think her mother would have preferred she had chosen a good Scotsman closer to home.

21
Chapter

For quite some time, our town had become a place for a stopover on the way to the South. Businesses were moving North, and we were becoming a second-rate town. The local Chamber of Commerce sent a trade delegation to America to examine how they had turned around a town there with a similar problem, and they returned with creative ideas. Up until then, the local Council had a very traditional outlook and did not like change. A large public meeting was arranged in the Town Hall, and a steering committee was founded. At a similar meeting in America, it was discovered that barbeque beef was the most popular commodity they produced, and so they organised huge competitions and festivals encouraging barbeque cooks from all over the States to participate. The public meeting in the Town Hall was to discover what was our strength to encourage people to live and work here. After heated exchanges and arguments from the floor, and with the committee on stage obviously hoping for their own prearranged ideas to be acknowledged, we were divided into groups. I chose the Business group.

My sister and I had agreed beforehand what we were interested in pursuing. We both thought our location was ideally situated to become a Health Spa city. It was close to surfing beaches and within easy reach of thermal springs and the Alps, with ski fields galore. Various engineering and plastic surgery specialists could combine to develop a variety of prostheses. The geology of the countryside was ideal for growing herbs and roses, so herbal remedies and perfumery was another suggestion. Wild flower seeds could also be distributed along road verges, and collections could be sold to tourists at airports. Vineyards that were just becoming popular on the Peninsular could be encouraged. There could be an Agribusiness Centre and a data collection building in the centre of town, where farmers and business people could communicate globally.

I considered our main advantage was our totally pure artesian water that most residents took for granted. It had no minerals in it, came from deep aquifers stored beneath the shingle beds, and was fed with mountain snow melt emanating from the Antarctic. There were also untapped thermal springs nearby at a market garden that were used to heat the house and greenhouses, as well as at a harbour village where the spring flowed onto the beach. The possibilities surrounding these projects were endless.

The business group took a whole year to discuss what our mission statement should be. We were issued with planning schedules, and I quietly got on with researching my project. I tried to find a Maori elder who would help me find a focal point for my idea. I researched possible depths of aquifers with the water engineers, who were more than excited about the project. They felt the emphasis on water conservation and care very overdue. Drawing attention to the unique aquifers was worth supporting. With continual stops and starts caused by our chairperson resigning and my Maori elder dying, it was another year before anything got off the ground.

A new person offered his help, and after appealing to Uenuku, the tribal rainbow warrior god, my project suddenly took on a life of its own. I founded Triskele Foundation as president to raise funds and oversee the project, employing two sculptors, a fabric artist, a graphic artist, a studio potter, and a model maker. A young man was co-opted to help with applying for support from various grants. I approached the Curator of the Botanic Gardens to choose a suitable site to create an installation in homage to the settlers, the resident Maori tribe, and their shared belief in the healing qualities of the pure water. An old Victorian drinking fountain had been placed near a capped artesian spring by the water gardens. The ambience surrounding it was tranquil and seemed ideal. This was the place. We held Drinks on the Lawn beside the water gardens to celebrate, using a local caterer and fruit-flavoured water from a local bottling company.

My assistant and I designed a glossy promotional booklet and approached various organisations willing to sponsor us. The Council landscape designer and I scoured the volcanic hills on the Peninsular for suitable rocks for a pool. A special large rock was chosen from which water would magically spout, providing the source for tasting the spring water. The spring came from very far down below the earth, and if left uncapped, the geyser would have gushed as high as the surrounding tall trees. We decided to call it Te Puna Ora, or the Spring of Life. A monumental mason gave us two very large blocks of Portland stone that had been in their yard for a long while. I had the two sculptors carve a copy of the triskelion found at Newgrange and the Maori Kaitiaki Kiwa from the blocks of Portland stone. A storyteller was chosen to introduce visitors to the spring, and the textile artist made silk cloaks for her and the Maori musician who would accompany her. The potter made stoneware goblets and sake bottles as keepsakes to be sold at the Information Centre. A local artist gave us some huge panels he had painted of the triskelion to stand in the storyteller's office. In later years, both the cloaks and the paintings disappeared.

About the same time, a local historian was writing beautifully illustrated books on Maori legend and culture. *Song of the Stone* had been a great success, and he was in the process of writing *Song of Waitaha*, which traced the tribe's origins to three areas around the Pacific Ocean, giving them a multicultural heritage. They were called the Rainbow people, with their rainbow warrior god Uenuku as their guide. The Waitaha had made landfall at a place we knew as Castle Rock in Canterbury, tying their canoe's anchor to the navigation star above. The author was told by the Elders to visit an American Indian tribe and present them with a piece of greenstone. This meeting provided him with greater spiritual insights that explained their deep understanding and relationship with the cosmos. He had visited the tribe, but incredibly the tribe had come to visit me. This became more poignant at the Dawn Ceremony to lift the Tapu on the spring.

The tohunga and members of the Waitaha tribe gathered on the bridge over the River Avon with our party just before dawn on the Spring Equinox of 1992 while he explained the order of service. He said the area I had chosen to create Te Puna Ora had originally been a sanctuary for women, and because of the mixture of the Waitaha ancestors, it was a remarkable coincidence that a woman from an overseas ancestry had rekindled it. It was a very important place historically and spiritually. After the ceremony, Te Puna Ora was opened to the public, and as the spring water was shared with guests, a rainbow was seen touching the pond through a parting of tree branches above.

22

My daughter and my daughter-in-law had more children. My daughter had another girl, and my daughter-in-law had a boy. My youngest son and fiancée returned to Scotland, and at sixty-four I was considering retirement. I still decorated my house for Christmas and enjoyed the lead-up with the pleasure of choosing gifts. Sometimes I had Christmas dinner with my older son and his family, and sometimes I had it with my friends, but my daughter always tugged at my heart. I had parties on the sundecks during the holidays and afternoon tea with my sister in the atrium of a prestigious hotel. These were fancy affairs with cakes and sandwiches on wood side stands, and silver service with a waiter pouring the tea. It harked back to a more graceful period with a concert pianist playing soft music on a piano in the centre of the floor. The space was surrounded by tiers of plant-filled verandas, and the outside lift moved up and down, with the occupants viewing the scene below.

My English Setter was ailing, and eventually I had to have him euthanised. He had cancer of the liver. I had not realised he was so ill, and the stays in kennels while I went overseas proved too much for him. It was far more traumatising than I had expected. I can still see his surprised face as he sat in the vet's station wagon, being driven to the surgery. It was the last I saw of him. I think it was far worse than losing a loved person. My next-door neighbour had lost her husband, and she had a Golden Labrador called Sandy. I did not have a car anymore, and she could not drive, so I used to take her for drives. When she died, Sandy decided to live with me. I still had a ginger cat who was ageing. My Mother had died and left her house to me and my sister. I had a conservatory built on the front of my house, and I wandered around my cliff garden and the two sundecks thinking that this property should be for a family, not just for one person. I began to look at other possibilities.

My daughter was pregnant again and wanted me to come over for the birth in August 1994. She and her husband and two girls had moved to a village in Dorset. They were in the process of converting two cottages into one, and once again chaos reigned. I arranged for a lady to house-sit for me and look after Sandy. I had put him in kennels during my last trip, and he had barked himself hoarse. My grandson was born two days after my birthday amidst great excitement. I helped look after the family as best I could, and not long afterwards, my son-in-law was posted to a job up in Oxfordshire. I took the girls to play school and babysat while my daughter was busy. It was obvious that the children needed a grandmother, so when my daughter wrote saying that she wished I was nearby permanently, I made plans to return to Dorset the following year. This time it was for good.

Although it was not an easy decision to make, leaving everyone dear to me behind, I began slowly downsizing the contents of my home by arranging the odd garage sale of items, taking books to the library and schools for them to keep or sell, and advertising pieces of furniture in the local newspaper. I gave odd bits away and auctioned some pieces. I went through all my albums of photographs and my artwork and burned those I did not need. The ashes were dug into the ground outside the back door. When I had finally sorted what furniture and household items to keep, I put the house up for sale with a local agent. After fourteen years, the house was worth three times more. The place sold within three months, by which time I had a well-known carrier come to pack and crate the whole contents for shipment to Britain. The cost included storage until I was ready to receive the goods.

The author of *Song of the Stone* came in person to deliver the second edition of his book *Song of Waitaha*. He brought me a sliver of pounamu greenstone from a river on the West Coast that he said had the water running through it. It was a sacred stone valued highly for its hardness and deep spiritual quality. I was told to keep it close to my heart; it would heal my body and bring me back to the Land. He also handed me a letter thanking me for bringing Te Puna Ora back to life.

After bidding a fond farewell to my family and friends and promising to visit in two years, it was time to leave. I had lived thirty-five years in New Zealand. I left in the winter and arrived in England three days later in the summer, in time for my grandson's first birthday. With a mixture of joy and sadness, I began a new life once more. I was homeless again, but I sent my guardian angel on ahead with instructions to find a suitable home for me close to my daughter and her children.

23
Chapter

If I had imagined that life was going to be simpler, I was mistaken. In 1995 at the age of sixty-six, I decided to retire back to Britain and live close to my family. After looking at various possible venues, my daughter showed me a cottage just down the hill from where she lived. It was one of four Georgian terrace farm cottages right on the village main road, near to town. It was no longer on the market, so we arranged to meet the owner. I fell in love with it immediately. It was the perfect Christmas cottage, with an inglenook fireplace, inset bread oven, window seats, and oak beams. Certainly it needed a lot of cosmetic work, filling in woodworm holes and cracks, and a bit of paint here and there, but the possibilities were endless. I bought the cottage outright for cash, with some funds left over for improvements. Although my household goods were still in store, I moved in right away.

By a curious coincidence, the main road was closed to traffic because of repairs when the huge furniture van squeezed its way down the narrow country main road. In the distant past, the road had been a carriageway to Sherbourne, with a change of horses being made just down the lane at a local farm. The van driver dumped the large boxes in the sitting room and left, leaving me to unpack. What joy to see all my belongings again, and it was miraculous that they were all in one piece. Everything fitted into the cottage setting. My pictures, furniture, and four-poster bed were made for it. The little nooks begged for precious pieces and books. It was as if all my previous life had been in preparation for this place.

There are a lot of books about interior decorating, but making a house into a home is a special trick. The Scandinavians call it hygge. I learned a lot from my parents on the arrangement and choice of eclectic pieces, but the real science had to do with welcome and comfort rather than displayed wealth. My cottage had hygge. The walls cuddled me. I had bookshelves made by a friend in cottage style. I wallpapered and painted, filled holes, and had damp-proofing done. At Christmas I turned my home into a sparkling grotto, hanging beautifully made baubles from the rafters and fairy lights and tinsel swags around the inglenook. I bought an artificial Christmas tree instead of a live one to avoid pine needles dropping on the floor, and I dressed it in decorations bought from a wonderful garden centre. It stood nicely on the window seat in the sitting room with a small decorative lamp containing an orange bulb on the dining alcove window sill. People passing in the street outside said how wonderfully festive it looked with the table set for Christmas Eve supper.

Because my daughter lived on top of a steep hill and I could not easily carry their gifts, I revived an old custom of entertaining on Christmas Eve. I provided a supper of cold collations that included turkey and ham pie, smoked trout, and varieties of cheeses and salads. Pavlovas and fruit salad followed with lashings of cream. Presents were given out to unwrap or save for the following day. I often bought a Christmas pudding but hardly ate any of it and saved it for Easter. Food was so readily available in the supermarket the making of the pudding was no longer a family affair. My daughter made her Christmas cake, but that too became a memory.

During the chilly autumn, I transformed the strip of field grass at the back of the cottage into a cottage garden. The cottages had been purpose-built by the farmer for his daughters in the late 1700s, and originally twelve acres of land had been attached to them. There was now a boundary wall where outside toilets had been, with access to a well at the bottom of the strip. Beyond were water meadows down to the river by the side of a lane. Horses grazed on a steep hill up to a ridgeway. In the deep past, this was a path where ancient people herded cattle when the valley flooded. I dug out a pond and a winding path and made a patio out of the top of the old septic tank. I planted fruit trees and cottage garden plants and made a circular lawn. My daughter and I collected Chesil Beach stones to spread on the path, filling hessian sacks until the back of her car dragged on the ground. In summer, I sat on the lawn beneath the trees and watched the swallows darting to catch bugs and the hoverflies vying with bumblebees for nectar from the blossoms. It became a haven for wild creatures. Weeds grew up alongside cultivated shrubs and roses. Frogs and newts with hovering dragonflies inhabited the pond. It was an idyllic paradise.

Although the Christmas carnival did not start until early December, the shops were full of Christmas goodies and cards in October. It was essential to send parcels overseas by the end of October. Christmas office parties began at the beginning of November, and schools prepared for end-of-year festivities with Nativity plays and open classrooms. Christmas markets and craft fairs were full of wonderful art and handwork. Wreaths of holly and mistletoe, Christmas lilies, and Norway spruce trees lined the market stalls, along with fruits, cheeses, pies, and meats from market farmers. A huge decorated tree was set up in the marketplace, ready for the carnival.

The carnival band, dressed like clowns with fake bottoms hanging out of their baggy pants, paraded down the street, followed by a motley crowd of children and adults in floats depicting fairy tales. The parade continued with dancing girls and strutting soldiers, causing a sensation, with the crowd clapping and tossing coins. My grandchildren were on one of the floats, and we waved excitedly as they passed by. Almost all the shops appeared to offer mince pies and mulled wine by assistants dressed in a range of costumes. A hog roast drew a large crowd of hungry visitors. Father Christmas, in his carriage drawn by ponies trotted past and then, all too soon, it ended. A fun fair in the big market place drew the crowd while groups of people dressed in Victorian costume entertained with carols in the various arcades. The weather turned very cold, and a few spots of snow fell that first Christmas at home.

The village church was decorated with greenery plucked from village gardens as we attended the carols by candlelight on Christmas Eve. After a family dinner with my daughter, son-in-law, and grandchildren excitedly opening their presents on Christmas Day, Boxing Day walk across country fields and footpaths was a welcome treat. Lots of people joined us as we ended the walk at a country inn. Dogs, muddy-booted walkers, and squabbling children jostled for space next to the roaring wood fire. A large, decorated Christmas tree stood near the entrance to welcome visitors. The bar, crowded with Dorset locals, buzzed with activity. We ordered cider with a plate of fries to share. We were invited to a party in the evening given by a family friend. She always provided a sumptuous table of food, and while it was being made, we had full range of the house, trying to find clues in a treasure hunt. There were more games after the meal and small gifts for the children.

True to tradition, Christmas lasted until Twelfth Night, when I decided to have a Wassail party for family and friends. My invited guests were asked to bring a bottle of cider as well as wine and a plate of something made with apples or apple juice. I bought a plucked pheasant for a cider casserole dish, but the butcher forgot to pick out the lead pellets from the carcass; this was not discovered until after it was served. After a hearty meal, we traipsed into the garden, poured cider on the apple trees, put a piece of toast on the branches of each one, and banged on saucepan lids to scare the unwanted spirits from the trees—as well as annoying neighbours. This ancient custom apparently ensured a good harvest the following autumn. We drank cider punch and ate Dorset apple cake, sang the Wassail song, and told stories by the log burner. Before they left, some of the guests helped to take down the decorations and dismantle the tree. This was to be the setting for Christmas for many years to come, but events intervened again to put a twist in my story.

24
Chapter

For quite a while before I returned to Britain, I had noticed a jabbing pain in my right breast. I was already in the throes of planning to move and so decided to ignore it. Now I began to see that my breast was forming a dimple close to the nipple, and I realised I had a tumour. I was not going to do anything until one day I slipped on a sandy step going down to the beach and broke my ankle. I had not wanted to have any more surgery, but I was being forced to have a steel pin put in my leg to support the ankle. I was hospitalised for several weeks after contracting a resistant viral infection. In October 1966, I was diagnosed with breast cancer and had a mastectomy. I was put on an oral chemotherapy for three years that completely lulled my libido. Although there were numerous causes for this type of cancer, hormone therapy was one of them. Recovery was painful and emotionally distressing. I was able to get compensation for breaking my ankle on a public path. I bought a tabletop computer and began writing my life stories.

I joined the Country Women's Institute, formed art classes and an embroidery group, and made a millennial tablecloth. At the local school, I helped the first-year children learn how to use a computer and I helped look after my grandchildren. I tried to form a discussion group similar to the one I'd belonged to previously, without much success. My sister came to stay for Christmas one year and was delighted with all the festivities surrounding the event. Several friends made trips to visit me from New Zealand, and we spent perhaps the coldest ever midsummer evening shrouded in clouds on top of an Iron Age hill fort to watch the sun go down.

My two sons came to visit. The youngest one was now married, and he returned with his wife to New Zealand and then went to Australia to live. They had a girl and a boy. The eldest now had three children, the last a boy. I took each of my three grandchildren in Britain to visit their cousins in New Zealand and Australia. Through a dear friend of the family who worked on the greens for the films, we were fortunate to go on the set of *King Kong* and see the places where *Lord of the Rings* was made. I was asked to become an Artist in Residence at the local school to design and make a mosaic River of Life pavement for a millennial project. I invited the children and parents to help, and we had great fun making the patterns, breaking up crockery, and collecting stones for filling gaps.

Coming up to Christmas 2007, I had been busy clearing the garden and putting the plants to bed. My sixteen-year-old grandson had put up the artificial Christmas tree and helped decorate the house. The wood burner was alight in the inglenook, and I was alone and relaxed, watching an episode of *Cranford* on the television. As I stood up to make myself supper, my left leg gave way, and I fell on the floor. I was unable to get up again. My left arm had lost strength as well. I managed to drag myself to the telephone to call my daughter, and soon I was being rushed to hospital in an ambulance. I was having a heart attack and a stroke. I grew old overnight.

26
Chapter

By the time I reached accident and emergency, the whole of my left side was completely paralysed and felt like a lump of lead. A searing pain pierced my right side under my shoulder blade, and although I could breathe in, I had to force my breath out, making guttural panting noises. I was very close to death and wondered where God was in all of this. I told God to either take me or heal me. The staff told me later that they had never seen such a quick recovery. Although I assured them that it was due to the Holy Spirit, I was told that the healing came from the patients themselves.

The medics went through their repertoire, taking electrocardiogram readings, inserting tubes, asking lots of questions, and rushing me into the waiting rooms on a stretcher. My daughter sat beside me with a few belongings, thinking I was only going to be there for a few hours. I was in hospital for months. Although this appeared to happen suddenly, there had been previous warnings with a pain behind my right shoulder blade, a dry cough, and shortness of breath months beforehand. I had sought medical advice and been told I had extreme heart failure. It was treated with medication. After a slow and painful recovery, I was able to learn how to walk with a stick, but my left side remained weak.

Patients in the Stroke Recovery ward lined each side of the room, with various tubes and wires linking them to machines and monitors that beeped and whistled. The cacophony of noise was deafening. The patients, in various stages of recovery, were very elderly with heads and hands poking over the hospital blankets like baby birds on a branch. Others like me had recovered fairly quickly to the extent that we could sit up and manoeuvre into a wheelchair. I had found the whole experience surreal. I had never experienced anything vaguely similar in my life, and it struck me as incredibly funny. My left arm had a life of its own and suddenly twitched like Peter Sellers's character Doctor Strangelove. My daughter brought me a black glove to put on my wayward hand as a joke. Like a naughty toddler, my hand scrunched up as soon as I tried to put it on.

Christmas music was piped through on the hospital radio. The staff had decorated the corridors with artificial holly. No flowers or plants were allowed in the ward, so my daughter brought in a colourful bunch of artificial Christmas arrangements. She read out greetings cards and letters and unpacked parcels. I could hardly make any sense of anything, but it was fun just the same. A large artificial tree had been unpacked and put in the community room on the ward. I was wheeled to a table nicely set with a colourful cloth and Christmas crackers to pull. We enjoyed a roast turkey meal and a small Christmas pudding with custard. I wondered what might be in the staff refrigerator and persuaded a nurse to have a look. She came back with a box of chocolates and a few bottles of beer. We all had upset stomachs the next day.

I was finally allowed home at Easter the following year. My sweet cottage had been slightly altered to accommodate a disabled person. I lived on my own, so it was imperative that I gain strength and the ability to look after myself. I reasoned that if my right side worked properly, then my left side could be taught to do the same. My brain had to make other connections to compensate for the part that had been damaged by a blood clot. To keep my brain active, I solved word puzzles and jigsaw puzzles. I wrote stories and poetry and painted pictures. I worked in the garden and joined a community embroidery group that was working on a town tapestry. I designed, painted, and embroidered various scenes in the tapestry panels that are now hanging in the Town Hall. A group of us continued to work on community projects and made several tapestries, cushions for dignitaries, church hangings and vestments, and a waistcoat for the Town Crier.

The following year, I began to suffer from occasional blackouts. I also had vivid hallucinations. I had always seen things from an early age, but now it was such an amazing parade of people and objects that I made an album of what I saw. My son from Australia was visiting with his family when I blacked out and fell backwards down the stairs. Once more I was rushed to hospital, where eventually it was agreed I had severe heart failure and required a pacemaker. An implanted cardiac defibrillator was installed. If my heart failed, I got an electric shock to start it again. It was obvious I could no longer remain in my cottage, and a modern retirement flat was found for me in the purpose-built village farther down the road.

All my cottage furniture looked out of place in the modern setting, and I had to replace it. While downsizing once more with the help of my New Zealand son, I took up residence and bought a mobility scooter that took apart to be packed in the back of a car. I could go shopping at the local store and go out with my daughter without her having to push a wheelchair. I continued to be monitored by the Cardiology Department at the hospital, and I employed a cleaner to help tidy my flat.

The building had a large community room that had originally been designed as a restaurant for the residents. It seemed an ideal location for a charity tea party. A few of the residents and I sent out invitations to friends and relatives, including the flat dwellers. I suggested we open our apartments and decorate the corridor for the event. We each provided home-made cakes and sandwiches and set up tables in one of the larger sitting rooms. It was a great success, and we made a good profit.

A large chestnut tree grew on the border of the property. My second-floor balcony overlooked the glorious parkland garden of the old Victorian mental hospital now converted into apartments. Rooks built their tenements in the ancient beech and sycamore trees surrounding the building. The chestnut tree was in glorious full bloom when it was decided to fell it because of a beetle infestation that killed the leaves. I planted some daffodil bulbs by its stump, and that encouraged others to begin planting around it. A community garden sprung up, and soon the border was cleared of builder's rubble and a shrubbery was planted. We formed a gardening club to beautify the surroundings, and it became a lovely place to sit beneath the tall trees.

I lived at the retirement establishment for about five years, during which time I discovered a tumour in my left breast. In 2013 I had another mastectomy. I had always looked after my body, taking care that I had a healthy diet, did not smoke or drink, and did regular exercise. I enjoyed dancing and yoga, power walking, and qigong, so my body was in good trim. It was now beginning to look like a patchwork quilt on an unmade bed. Undaunted, I continued to visit my sons and their families in Australia and New Zealand, and I took my grandson once more to visit his cousins in Australia. My sons carried on our love of parties and my youngest son gave a large family reunion party in my honour. Upon returning to Britain, I discovered that the owner of the retirement building was selling the property; all the people renting their flats had to leave within the month. My daughter and I scoured the advertisements in estate agents' windows without success. We went to see several places that looked promising, but they were very expensive to rent. It had been agreed that because I was now well into my eighties, it was foolish to buy another property. The time to leave was fast approaching, and I had not found somewhere else to live. I wondered where I would be next Christmas.

27
Chapter

I asked my guardian angel to find me somewhere suitable. I tried to be specific in describing what and where I preferred to live. It had to be accessible for a mobility scooter, have a courtyard where I could sit in the sun, and have a small garden to potter in and grow plants. It had to have two bedrooms in case I needed overnight care, must be within easy reach of shops and town, and must have a large dining kitchen. We had registered with all the estate agents except one. While we were walking down the high street one afternoon, an agent from this company accosted us in the street. She said she had heard that we were looking for a place, and she had the perfect one for me. It was not on the market yet, but we could go to see it. It was exactly as I had described.

The stone house had been a manor farm, probably built in the late 1700s and converted into two flats. It shared a large courtyard with garages and a block of flats, right next door to a vast Victorian manse that was now a halfway house. Opposite, an ancient Norman church built on a Saxon royal chapel rang its bells every Sunday, reminding parishioners to attend the service. I had been attending the Baptist church in town, but now there was no excuse to not go to church here. I was made most welcome and joined several groups, including a lunch club for the elderly of the parish. There was a village green and a community field where a beacon stood and where people walked their dogs. An ancient hill fort rampart had been converted into the boundary walls of a Roman fortress and was now a tree-lined walkway for pedestrians. I went along the walks on my mobility scooter to go into town to shop.

The grandchildren were now adults. Whether married or with partners, they were scattered all over the world. It seemed curious to be celebrating festive occasions with only my daughter for company. I sent parcels of lucky dip gifts for overseas families, and when they grew older, I went online and ordered hampers to be dispatched from Australian and New Zealand suppliers.

I have enjoyed five years in this stone house with its farmhouse kitchen and spacious sitting room. It is ideal for entertaining although most of my friends have passed on. One of my granddaughters came to stay shortly after I moved here, and my grandson came to stay with his girlfriend for a while. I still decorate my room at Christmas but now have a fibre-optic tree. I gave my families the baubles I collected over the years for them to enjoy.

Last year, I went to Australia for a wedding; this year, my son in New Zealand invited me for Christmas. It was one continuous party lasting several weeks and ending with a spectacular wedding in a vineyard. New Zealand has changed a lot since we first arrived as immigrants. There is a female Prime Minister, for a start. The country is full of immigrants from all around the world, and the Maori language is displayed openly on signage and documents; their culture has been adopted as part of the accepted way of life. Since a disastrous period of earthquakes, the city is being rebuilt with extraordinary, strong monumental buildings defying the elements. Once upon a time, trees were topped and the land was cleared for farming, but now the land is sheltered by screens of tall trees, and vineyards cover pastures. Some forests are protected as national parks. Those areas that had buildings demolished in the seaside suburbs and around wetlands have been left as parkland now, and new areas are developed north of the city. My sons have flourished, and their families have grown to adulthood. Most of my old friends have passed on, and the houses I lived in were destroyed in the quakes.

I will be ninety in August 2019. I am planning a week celebration in a modern cottage in Devonshire. All are invited. Any excuse for a party.

Lightning Source UK Ltd.
Milton Keynes UK
UKHW010748041019
350967UK00001B/293/P